Dear Luke,

We need to

TALK.

—Darth

DEAR LUKE, WE NEED TO TALK.

—DARTH

AND OTHER POP CULTURE CORRESPONDENCES

JOHN MOE

Three Rivers Press • New York

Published in the United States by Three Rivers Press,
an imprint of the Crown Publishing Group,
a division of Penguin Random House LLC, New York.
threeriverspress.com

Earlier versions of "Concerning Jon Bon Jovi, wanted dead or alive," "Memo regarding changes to the Hotel California in light of Mr. Don Henley's recent complaint," "Notes on 'Sweet Child o' Mine,' as delivered to Axl Rose by his editor," "A note placed in the pay envelope of Billy 'The Piano Man' Joel," "A letter from The Power to Public Enemy," "A court-ordered letter from Dora the Explorer's mother," "A letter to Elvis Presley from his hound dog," "A midyear update from Miss Othmar," "A retort to Carly Simon regarding her charges of vanity," "A letter to Elton John from the office of the NASA Administrator," and "James Taylor issues an update on 'The Friendship Promise'" appeared on McSweeneys.net. An earlier version of "A letter to The Grinch following the events of a significant Christmas" appeared as a commentary on NPR.

Library of Congress Cataloging-in-Publication Data

Moe, John.
Dear Luke, we need to talk, Darth : and other pop culture
correspondences / John Moe. –First edition.
pages cm
1. Popular culture-Humor.   1. Title
PN6231.P635M64 2014
306.480973-dc23   2013045747

Proprietary ISBN: 978-0-385-36555-0

Printed in the United States of America

Domestically printed by Berryville Graphics

Proprietary Edition, 2017 Sterling

CONTENTS

Dear Luke,

We need to

TALK.

—Darth

CONCERNING JON BON JOVI,

WANTED

DEAD OR ALIVE

Attention, all law enforcement in the region:

I realize many of you have become cynical about the all-points
bulletins issued for dangerous criminals. I'm sure you think they're
essentially all the same and that only the names have changed. But I
urge you to pay close attention in your pursuit of Mr. Jon Bon Jovi.
He's wanted. Wanted dead or alive.

Who is Bon Jovi? Well, to begin with, he's a cowboy. Granted,
it's fairly routine for cowboys to run afoul of the law, especially in
the winter, when the work and money dry up and they've got time
on their hands. Plenty of petty theft, public intoxication, and lewd-
behavior calls. But that's not what we're up against. Bon Jovi is no
regular cowboy. He rides a horse made of steel. A steel horse.

I am not shitting you.

And don't think this is some sort of comical clunky robot horse
with whimsical hydraulic sound effects and extraneous flashing
lights. This thing is exactly like a thoroughbred, only much larger
and made from an incredibly resilient alloy. Bullets can't even
penetrate this horse, much less stop it. Bon Jovi is also armed with
a loaded six-string that he carries on his back. Reports differ on
whether he uses it as a sort of crossbow or whether it's actually a

guitar that he plays with such shocking mastery as to render victims helpless. Regardless, take heed.

There is other information I need to share with you about Bon Jovi. And no matter how callous you think you are to the attributes of criminals, you may want to brace yourself. Bon Jovi has almost superhuman abilities. Sure, sometimes he sleeps, but sometimes he can go for days without doing so. Days! To compensate for this interruption in his circadian rhythms, Bon Jovi has evidently crafted some sort of alcohol-based calendar, where he can actually tell the day by the bottle that he drinks.

So why are we looking for Bon Jovi? Why is he wanted, wanted dead or alive? A spree of face rocking. Estimates vary as to how many faces have been targeted—some say 800,000, some say 1.2 million—but it is accepted as a fact that he has rocked every single face he has seen. Every one of them. We're not even clear on a motive for this mass face rocking, although there are reports of Bon Jovi complaining of faces that "are so cold."

Will he stop at a million faces? How many will be enough? We can't afford to find out.

Now all this being said, if you should come in contact with Bon Jovi, do not look into his face. He will only rock your face. And call for backup immediately.

Good luck to you all. At this point, I have to be honest. We're living on a prayer.

Sincerely,
Sgt. H. Locklear

Bruce: A Shark's Journal

April 7

So this is the journal that I'm supposed to be writing in, as prescribed by my latest therapist. I hope it helps but I have to be honest, I doubt it will. I WANT TO STOP EATING EVERYONE! That's it! That's all I want! I've been through—what—five therapists now trying to fix this problem I have? And I've eaten three of those therapists. I can't form any meaningful relationships with anyone because sooner or later, CHOMP. It's got to stop. I want to do things. I want to get married. I want to swim up to a female and impregnate her. But for any of that to work, the killing simply has got to stop. And I'm nervous because summer is coming up. Maybe this summer will be different.

May 2

This summer WILL be different. THIS SUMMER MUST BE DIFFERENT!

May 12

How could the summer be different?! I'm a SHARK. A GREAT WHITE SHARK. A nonstop killing machine! NO! No. I am in control here. Biology is not destiny. I have to think positive. I can be any kind of nonstop machine I want to be. A nonstop caring machine. A nonstop listening machine. A nonstop nurturing machine.

May 31

Tourists are showing up. I ate kelp and seaweed today. I've read, like, three books this week just to keep my mind off things. Jacqueline Susann. Better than I expected.

June 14

Okay. Deep breath. I'm ashamed to even be writing this. But I fell off the wagon BIG TIME.

It was night and I was swimming around (I don't sleep), and I thought everything would be fine because what human would be out in the ocean at night? Then this lady shows up swimming around. Naked! Now, I'm not into human chicks in a sexual way—I'm not a perv or anything—but I see that and I'm thinking, "no nylon swimsuits, no goggles to deal with, just dinner."

I'm not blaming the victim here—I'M NOT—she has/had the right to swim wherever, whenever, wearing whatever she wanted. But I could not resist. And thus, chomp.

I was so disgusted with myself that I couldn't even eat all of her. I dumped her mangled remains on the beach, kind of as a way of saying sorry to the humans. I hope they were able to pick up on how contrite I was when they saw her carcass.

4

June 23

Guilt does funny things to a shark. When I feel guilty about something (like, oh, EATING A WOMAN), I start to hate myself. When I start to hate myself, I engage in self-destructive behavior. If I were a human (like the one I ATE), that might mean eating a bunch of ice cream or getting drunk. But I'm a shark and I dragged a boy from shore and ate him up. He was smaller than my previous meal, but, I don't know, it still doesn't feel like progress to me. It's like the only way I can feel good is to do bad?

June 26

There's no doubt about it: I'm spiraling. Sank a boat today. Ate the captain. Most of him anyway. Started innocently enough. I saw the boat out there on the water, and I remembered what I read in a self-help book: "use your tongue instead of your teeth." I figured I could swim up and talk to the guy about my issues. Maybe he could provide some help from a human perspective.

Then before I know it he's whapping me on the nose, which is NOT COOL, and one thing led to another. Suddenly I was on the attack. I need to remember that it's not enough to want to reach people. I have to understand how I'm coming across to them as well.

But why do all my conflicts end with eating people? Why is that always my end-game? Maybe because I'm a Great White Shark but I don't ACCEPT that destiny as an ABSOLUTE.

July 5

Ate another dude. Maybe I was still mad at the boat captain. Or mad at my mother who birthed me and then just swam away. Or mad at myself.

I also know that the people are on to me. They're upset. And they're coming for me and it's not to talk things over. You see what I've done here: I'VE TAUGHT THEM TO KILL. It's a cycle. Like, who's the real monster here? Is it me, the shark, or is it those people who want to kill me? Realistically, I know it's me. I wish it weren't.

July 7

Yeah, they're coming for me. I should just head out to the greater ocean and put Cape Cod behind me. Somehow I can't. I think I need closure. Whether that will come from eating every person who comes near the water or being harpooned I can't say. But I see their boat. Looks like there's an old sea captain, a sort of wild-eyed young researcher, and Roy Scheider on it. I'm going to them. One way or another, we're going to end this thing.

(JOURNAL ENDS)

JAY Z'S 99 PROBLEMS

1. Someone might figure out the *Z* stands for *Zippy*.
2. Missing *Golden Girls* DVD box set.
3. People pronouncing my name "Jaze."
4. Don't really enjoy rap music.
5. Rap patrol on gat patrol.
6. A bitch. Ha! Gotcha. No, just kidding. It's mosquitos.
7. Overall concern over the direction of the *Dr. Who* franchise.
8. Where to dump Hal Linden's body.
9. Ficus plant seems droopy.
10. Do I have enough sunglasses?
11. Is it possible to EVER have enough sunglasses?
12. If not, have I set myself up for a life without satisfaction where a thousand sunglasses will never be as good as two thousand sunglasses?
13. How can I go about buying all the sunglasses?
14. How do I persuade everyone else in the world to destroy or give me their sunglasses so no one else can ever have sunglasses?
15. These grapes taste weird.
16. Inconvenient money allergy.
17. Ventriloquism classes not going well. Can't nail the B sound.
18. Rap critics that say I'm money, cash, hoes.
19. The U.S. can't seriously compete in Olympic table tennis.
20. Hoses on the soda fountain that dispense champagne are getting all gummed up.
21. Are my shiny things as shiny as they could be?
22. How do I go about firing my shiny thing shiner?
23. Do I have a human resources person I need to talk to first?

24. How do I advertise for a new shiny things shiner? Craigslist? Seems wrong.

25. What kind of questions do you ask someone like that in an interview?

26. Pet tiger seems bored.

27. Other pet tiger unaccounted for (note: they don't really play fetch. Not in the classical sense.)

28. Have to get more gazelle for tiger(s), stocks running low.

29. Fools that want to make sure my casket's closed.

30. Martin Mull's a good actor. Why can't he get a series?

31. Beyoncé's former Destiny's Child bandmates still "crashing" in the rec room. It's been three months.

32. Chafing.

33. Art Garfunkel won't return my calls.

34. Might lose favorite rhyming dictionary someday and career will be over.

35. I'm rich, happily married, popular, and respected. I guess this is more a brag than a problem.

36. Potty mouth.

37. What if there's someone left in the world who doesn't know who I am?

38. The ending of *The Sopranos*.

39. The ending of *According to Jim*.

40. Music is fine, but should I have stayed in the crack-dealing business?

41. How much would it cost to shrink a rhino to the size of a small dog to keep as a pet?

42. Who can do that for me?

43. How do I get a hold of that rhino-shrinking person?

44. Could I give shrunken rhino pets as gifts to friends or is that presumptuous?

45. What would I name my shrunken rhino pet? "Killer"? "Tupac"? "Pointy"?

46. What if all my fans start shrinking down rhinos to copy me and then they can't take care of them and abandon them? Because that would be a lot of guilt on me for starting this thing.

47. Could I just have a rhino horn surgically grafted on to a dog? Might be easier.

48. Beyoncé isn't very supportive when it comes to my interest in exotic pets.

49. Toothpaste tubes look all ugly.

50. No one sells a toothpaste tube encrusted in diamonds.

51. Jerks at Crest don't take my ideas seriously.

52. Rap mags try and use my black ass so advertisers can give 'em more cash for ads.

53. Do I sometimes come across as a little arrogant to people?

54. Constant thoughts that I should go back and get my bachelor's degree just in case.

55. Shamrock Shake only available once a year.

56. Beyoncé might be too pretty all the time, if that's actually a thing.

57. Sometimes I don't know what's actually a thing.

58. No one's written a "These Are Things" book or made a "These Are Things" rap video.

59. Sucker MCs.

60. Tim Conway films only sporadically available on Blu-Ray.

61. Solid gold helicopter can't even get off the ground because it's too heavy.

62. Same with solid gold hovercraft.

63. Solid gold submarine sinks just fine, but can't get back up to surface without being pulled by a solid gold cable.

64. Purchased Argentina but I lack a real understanding of the country's politics and culture.

65. Started several wars with other South American nations modeled on rap beefs.

66. Responsible for the deaths of thousands of citizens.

67. After I resigned as President of Argentina, Justin Timberlake wouldn't accept the position no matter how nicely I asked.

68. Neither would Kanye.

69. Or DMX.

70. Or LeBron James.

71. Going to have to sell Argentina at a loss and play two or even three concerts to make back money.

72. Fear of ants (they don't have faces).

73. Can't get that "I Want My Baby Back" Chili's jingle out of my head.

74. Can't figure out a way to at least rap over it and release it as a single to pay for a new head.

75. Cat keeps looking at me weird.

76. Cat won't wear diamond-encrusted mask.

77. Am a werewolf.

78. Body may be rejecting transplanted spine made of gold.

79. Gold spine sometimes sets off alarms at airports.

80. Can't find a good novel to read. John Grisham just seems to be repeating himself.

81. The mumps.

82. Damn public radio pledge drives.

83. Subscription to *McSweeney's Quarterly* ran out and Dave Eggers never told me (will take it up with him at book club.)

84. Worry someone will discover that I'm secretly a member of Bon Iver.

85. Making sure Beyoncé and I buy Blue Ivy the right school.

86. Concerned that my daughter will feel like she has to go into entertainment like her parents. She can do anything she wants as long as she's the best in the world at it.

87. Giraffes sure look freaky. What if one gets into the house and chases me?

88. Can't find anyone to kill all the giraffes.

89. Can't find anyone to cover all the giraffes with thick black curtains.

90. Can't find anyone to affix electronic sensors to giraffes so that if they get too close to the house a big WHOOOOOP-WHOOOOOP sound goes off.

91. $-12x - 4 = -103$

92. Can't figure out bus schedule.

93. These hover beans don't work because I can't hover.

94. When I'm chewing the finest gum in the world–which costs $10,000 a stick–and someone asks me for a piece of gum and I give it to them and that's fine but maybe they don't appreciate how fancy and valuable that gum is.

95. Plot holes in *Gremlins* that I'm going to have to address before the feature film marionette reboot I'm directing.

96. Never going to out-cool Evel Knievel.

97. Robo-Jay android doppelgänger keeps malfunctioning, attacking fans.

98. Climate change.

99. Can't get the hang of Ultimate Frisbee.

Dear Glinda,

I am safely back home in Kansas now and wanted to take a moment
to drop you a line. It's funny: Kansas has kind of a reputation as
a boring place. Flat, featureless, tedious. And it is those things. In
many ways Kansas is awful. Everyone here is frankly pretty screwed
up. People can only take so much Dust Bowl, you know? But I will
say this for Kansas: at least there are no wicked witches trying to kill
me here. Repeatedly. And cackling over the proposition because my
imminent murder gives them such hysterically humorous joy.

Obviously, that was the challenge I faced in my recent trip to
Oz: supernatural beings trying to kill me for actions that were in no
way my fault. And Glinda, I will always remember what you told me
about going home just before I transported back to Kansas. "You've
always had the power, my dear," you said. "You've had it all along."

I think about that a lot now, Glinda, because it helps me crystal-
lize my feelings for you. I hate you. I had the power to go home all
along? From the point I put those slippers on my feet back in Munchkinland, I could have gone home? I could have avoided the death
threats, the flying monkey attacks, the near-fatal narcotic overdose
in the poppy fields (you know poppies are what they make heroin out
of, right?), the imprisonment by the witch from which I escaped only

12

as a result of pure luck? If I had just done that click-my-heels thing at the start, none of that would have happened.

And as I recall, Glinda, you were RIGHT THERE in Munchkinland and could have shared that important bit of information right there on the spot.

Fuck you, Glinda.

After you finally did tell me how easily I could have avoided all that mortal danger, Scarecrow even asked you why you didn't tell me before. You said I wouldn't have believed you. The hell I wouldn't. I had already landed in a strange world, committed manslaughter, was surrounded by munchkins, and visited by witches. I would have believed literally anything at that moment. Or at least tried anything.

But no, you said, I had to find out for myself. Again: fuck you. And fuck you once more. Apparently "finding out for myself" means forming relationships with scarecrows and metal men who have come to life, as well as Bert Lahr in a lion suit. None of that—NONE OF THAT—is my idea of a good time. I'm fucking sixteen years old and wandering the woods with those creeps? What the fuck is wrong with you, Glinda?

Yeah, Kansas at its very dullest at least has some vague principles of honesty and decency.

All that being said, I confess I do hope to return to Oz one day. Not to visit my traveling companions, mind you; they scared me. I hope whatever Satanic witchcraft animated and anthropomorphized them will wear off and they will be dead or otherwise obliterated. No, I hope to return so that I can somehow find a way to burn down your whole horrible world. Good witches, bad witches, Munchkin-land, Land of Oz, whatever other twisted villages and hamlets I come across, flying monkeys; the whole lot of it must be incinerated in the name of biblical justice.

That's right: I'm a Kansas girl from early-20th century America. My religion is strong and my God is a wrathful and powerful one who doesn't look kindly on "magic" and "witches." It's idolatry and it must be punished. I will lay waste to all of it and watch it burn.

I'm coming for you, Glinda. And so is Jesus. And so is pain.

Dorothy Motherfucking Gale

CENTRAL INTELLIGENCE AGENCY

WASHINGTON, D.C.

OFFICE OF THE DIRECTOR

UPDATES ISSUED BY SPECIAL AGENT "GILLIGAN" FROM ISLAND PROJECT

September 25, 1964

All details appear to be in order for the mission to begin tomorrow. I have spent the past several months performing a variety of charmingly dunderheaded stunts at the local marina as a means of endearing myself to Jonas Grumby, who captains the tour boat S.S. *Minnow*. Psych 101 stuff but he's a simple man. Last week, I offered to perform the duties of first mate on the *Minnow* for a wage that was dramatically lower than the industry standard. This, combined with the pleasing contrast of his perpetual blue shirt to my perpetual red shirt has landed me the job.

Other agents in the field have conspired to bring our test subjects to the boat tomorrow for a 3-hr tour (a three-hour tour). Unless I receive a cancellation signal by the time we sail, I'll assume the mission is a go.

Thank you for all your hard work.

SA Gilligan

* * *

September 26, 1964

Success. Our associates in the Department of Weather Manipulation provided what could only be described as a perfect storm, which, combined with the precision sabotage of the *Minnow*, has indeed left us on this desert isle, which is charted only on classified government maps. There's already talk of naming it Gilligan's Island. Damn right it's my island.

The final roster of study participants is as follows:

- Myself
- Jonas Grumby, who is referred to by all participants as "Skipper."
- Thurston Howell III, a millionaire industrialist whose participation in the experiment was approved by a secret cabal of ill-tempered board members of Howell Industries.
- Eunice "Lovey" Wentworth Howell, wife of the above.
- A grifter, con artist, and presumed sex addict, real name unknown, who has convinced everyone else that she is a movie star named Ginger Grant, even though no such movie star exists.
- Mary Ann Summers, a young woman from Kansas whom all the men on board agree is way hotter than "Ginger." All the men seem to think this ranking is very important though I'm not sure why.

- Professor Roy Hinkley of our own research team who, like myself, is operating undercover.

Subjects seem sanguine about being stranded, confident they will be rescued soon. They have no idea how wrong they are.

Hinkley and I are excited to learn how people will react in a close-knit situation.

* * *

January 3, 1965

Observation: when people believe they are stranded on an island (and not part of a highly monitored experiment sponsored by the Department of Defense, the Central Intelligence Agency, Harvard University, the Trilateral Commission, the Council on Foreign Relations, and Procter & Gamble), they are willing to suspend certain tenets of reality. For instance, no one questions why the Howells have a seemingly limitless supply of clothing even though they originally set out for a three-hour tour on a small boat. Even the Howells themselves seem oblivious here. I suppose rich people are simply used to things being easy for them. Thank you to operatives who have been supplying items from the Howells' own wardrobe.

Also, no one has questioned how an island less than three hours away from a Hawaii marina can be uncharted.

March 18, 1965

My work as experiment facilitator is becoming a strain. Though I can retreat to my own secret underground bunker from time to time to enjoy the comforts of civilization, I still feel burdened. I have a doctorate in behavioral psychology from Princeton in addition to several years as a military tactician on behalf of the government, yet I must play the role of bumbling fool.

Admittedly, the "Gilligan" character is useful: On numerous occasions, the experiment subjects have come close to figuring out how to get off the island, only to have those attempts scuttled by a series of staged bungles that I have executed. Fortunately, either through poor intellect or growing madness, no one has established a pattern and simply kept me away from the rescue attempt.

I do wonder, however, if I am truly Dr. Gilligan or the dunderheaded first mate Gilligan. When a man spends all of his time in character, does he not become that character?

I like bananas.

* * *

June 21, 1965

Professor Hinkley is no help at all. While I fully inhabit the role of the inept naif, he insists on displaying his intellectual acumen by constructing radios out of coconut shells and so forth. Fortunately, none of the subjects have asked him why, if he can make a coconut radio, can he not make a FUCKING RAFT? Or a patch for the *Minnow*?

Still undetermined: What makes the subjects so dim that they do not ask these simple questions themselves? Is there something in the water? Is it connected to my suspicion that the insects we see around here are the souls of people we have known and they are punishing me for my sins?

* * *

October 3, 1965

Have had little contact with research team in recent months. I keep forgetting to check in and also whether any of this is real. In the meantime, I've become quite close to test subjects. I confess to feeling great affection when Skipper calls me "Little Buddy." Intellectually, I recognize the moniker as belittling, but you learn to take what you can around here in terms of affection.

Island life is sexless. "Ginger" seems to constantly perform the role of sexpot nymphomaniac, but it is just that, a charade, and she never makes any real advances toward anyone. The Howells are in a sexless marriage. I'm not sure what Hinkley is up to. You'd think that, left on an island with nothing to do, people would screw all day long. No.

I masturbate almost constantly.

I also notice I'm not as intellectually sharp as I once was. I am less like Dr. William Gilligan, PhD, and more like dumb ol' Gilligan. I had to look up how to spell William.

* * *

December 20, 1965

No one swears. Ever.

* * *

July 19, 1967

I found a journal with a bunch of silly things written in it!

Here's what's really funny: They all appear to be written in my handwriting! Something about an experiment? I don't know what that means.

We almost got off the island and I screwed it all up again! Skipper chased me into the lagoon and hit me with his hat!

That keeps happening.

Coconuts for dinner.

* * *

April 21, 1973

Ate the Howells. It was time.

* * *

November 2, 1978

My crown is fashioned from the head of Skipper. At least from the last earthly

form Skipper took. Skipper is god, Skipper is god.

I am new ruler of island. I am commander of monkeys. I am Gilligan. I am

Skipper's chosen vessel.

Evil force lives on other side of island. Mariannnn and Perfesser and there

children.

All uthers dead.

* * *

Gilligan 90, 19 Gilligan

Gilligan.

I will have vengeance.

Hotel California *"Such a Lovely Place"*

Dark Desert Highway, California

To: All staff

From: Management

As many of you know, our hotel recently hosted notable musician Don Henley. I wish I could say things went well but they did not. Mr. Henley registered his dissatisfaction not only in a letter to me but in a song that is fast on the way to becoming a classic rock staple, bound to be in heavy radio rotation for decades to come. And I fear that it will NOT help us attract new guests, aside from the occasional customer wondering if our hotel could really be as bad as it has been described to be.

We can't go back in time and change things, but we can demonstrate that we know how to make adjustments to make our guests more comfortable.

Here is the list of changes to come:

- **Update room décor.** This applies especially to the ceiling mirrors, which will be removed.

- **Restock alcohol supplies.** Encourage Captain to offer guests other options when a particular spirit or wine is unavailable. Do not simply say that we have not had that particular variety in many years and hang up the phone.

- **Acquire steelier knives and/or less resolute beast.**
We should be doing as little stabbing as possible, you guys.
I would like to explore the idea of maybe not even using live
beasts that need to be stabbed to death in the restaurant. The
time may have arrived to simply purchase meat like everyone
else does.

- **Emphasize "heaven" image over less desirable
"hell" alternative.** This is way overdue and dates back to
a decorating dispute at the founding of the hotel. The Hotel
California, as you know, was a joint project between the
Catholic Archdiocese and the Church of Satan. After all these
years of guests being unsure about theme, we should pick
one. Heaven. No one wants to sleep in hell.

- **Install electric-light system in hallway.** The candles
used by bellhops are supposed to be cool and mystical but
they're just weird. Let's just put some fluorescents up there.

- **Discontinue recorded announcements.** This includes
voices down the corridor welcoming guests to the Hotel
California, as well as the voices who wake guests up in the
middle of the night just to say "Welcome" once more. No one
likes this practice and we will stop it. There are better ways to
make guests feel welcome.

- **Upgrade music selection.** Keep in mind that some
guests dance to remember and others do so to forget. Neither
practice works, of course, but we should have some variety.

- **Improve courtyard air conditioning.** We ought to try to
reduce occurrences of sweet summer sweat. Gross.

- **Encourage nightman to be less cryptic when talking to guests.** Apparently the nightman told Mr. Henley to relax and that we are "programmed to receive." What does that even mean? Just be friendly. And no more quaaludes, folks. I'm serious this time.

- **Clearly mark passage back to places guests have been before.** No one likes being lost. A few signs would be nice.

- **Emphasize core strengths in our marketing.** Our hotel is a lovely place, there's always plenty of room, and any time of year, you can find us here. The hotel doesn't move around from place to place. Granted, no hotels do, but we should make the most of our limited selling points.

- **Provide "house alibis" to guests who neglect to bring their own.** Apparently Mr. Henley thought it important to remind people to bring their alibis. If a guest forgets a toothbrush, we always have some at the front desk. We should do the same here. Why would someone need an alibi? That's none of our business.

- **Streamline checkout procedures to accommodate guests' desire to actually leave.** Honestly, why is this even necessary to point out? I regularly find stock rooms full of unhappy guests when I come in to work in the morning. Just let them leave when they check out!

MINUTES FROM 9/12/99 ALL-DINOSAUR MEETING

PRESIDENT JEFF MARTIN (TYRANNOSAURUS REX)
called the meeting to order at 7:00 p.m. precisely.

PRESIDENT MARTIN's remarks:
"First of all, I want to thank everyone here for electing me to the
position of President of the Business Development Council. I know
that I have that 'Rex' in my name and a bit of a reputation but you
still didn't have to vote for me. I hope I earned your votes through my
dedication and intellect, not just the threat of me eating you."

NANCY KENDRICKS (COMPSOGNATHUS) asks if she would
have been eaten had she voted for, say, one of the Stegosauruses.

PRESIDENT MARTIN simply smiles and continues
his remarks:
"The purpose of this council is to figure out how to accomplish
something that Mr. John Hammond–all hail The Creator–never could:
how to open the gates of Jurassic Park for tourism. And to do that with
dinosaurs running the place. There are several challenges on the way

to accomplishing this goal, but I think most of us would agree that the rewards would be considerable."

PRESIDENT MARTIN asks the dinosaurs in attendance if anyone has any objections to pursuing this objective.

ART LAWSON (TROODON) raises a spindly arm and is called upon:
"Jeff, thank you for providing this forum. Now, we Troodons aren't as large as some of you, but there are a lot of us. Ours has been a very successful species and unlike some of those in attendance this evening, we have found no trouble procreating or finding food. For whatever reason, we do well."

A shout of "Racist" is heard from the back of the room. President Martin gavels the room to order with his comically tiny, almost useless arm.

MR. LAWSON continues.
"So I think this is an unnecessary and dangerous step. We're finding plenty to eat among the sick and old among the rest of you guys. And your babies. Nothing personal. And you'll recall the other times people have come here, it didn't work out too well. Lots of violence."

JENNIFER PORTER (VELOCIRAPTOR) hisses loudly and is called upon:
"From my species' vantage point, people visiting the island has worked out really great. You guys know what people are made of, right? Meat. They are fresh meat walking around. You unwrap them by taking their clothes off and they're just all meat. Along the way, some of our pack

died but since we're incapable of feelings of loss and grief that's no big deal. We say open the place and bring on the meat!"

Hisses of approval from Velociraptor section of the auditorium.

PRESIDENT MARTIN speaks:
"Jennifer brings up what I think is a really good point. You see, I've been thinking about this a lot. Which is hard, given the size of MY brain! [general laughter in the room] And the goal shouldn't be to eat the actual people who come to visit [boos from the room, hisses from the Velociraptors]. Now now, hear me out, folks. If we can open this business and if it can be US running the business, then maybe we can get something more than meat out of the arrangement. Maybe we can all acquire a little something called 'independence.' Now, I love Mr. Hammond—all hail The Creator—but a 'Jurassic Park' run by people just makes those people successful and profitable, all the while making us, the dinosaurs, indentured servants. And there wouldn't be a park if it weren't for us! If, on the other hand, we're doing the marketing, the accounting, the transportation, all the day-to-day operations of the park, then we're really running our own show."

GUS MATTHEWS (STEGOSAURUS) laboriously raises a leg:
"But that doesn't leave any time for roaming around grazing on plants."

MARY STEIN (MAIASAURA) speaks up:
"I think what Jeff is saying is that we get money from the people and then trade it for food and other things. Jeff, am I getting that right?"

PRESIDENT MARTIN replies:
"Yes! Precisely. They give us money, then we buy livestock for the

predators—they're totally delicious, you guys—and vegetation for the herbivores. You don't even have to hunt or look around for it. It's right there."

DON RUPRECHT (PACHYCEPHALOSAURUS) speaks up:
"Whoa, whoa, Jeff. You're losing me, dude. Under this scenario, I understand that we eat something called 'money,' but then how do we decide who among the dinosaurs are going to be killed and eaten?"

PRESIDENT MARTIN replies:
"Don, I'm sorry. Maybe I'm not making myself clear—"

MR. RUPRECHT replies:
"Or maybe you are. I wouldn't know, I run into things with my head all day. So . . ."

PRESIDENT MARTIN replies:
"I've written up a pamphlet on the whole system. Can anyone here read? Anyone? No? Okay, well, I've got a PowerPoint I can show in a little while."

MS. PORTER (VELOCIRAPTOR):
"What Jeff is saying is that we bring the people here, we take their money, we show them around, they have a great time—"

PRESIDENT MARTIN:
"Yes. Thank you, Jennifer."

MS. PORTER:

"And then we eat them."

PRESIDENT MARTIN:

"No!"

SANDY O'NEIL (TRICERATOPS):

"I think a lot of this sounds really interesting and I can totally get behind the idea of us not eating each other. I'm an herbivore, but I'd rather not impale those of you who try to eat me. I don't enjoy that and it is messy. My objection is with the name *Jurassic Park*. My ancestors weren't Jurassic, they were from the late Cretaceous. If people come here and think that I'm a Jurassic, I would be pretty embarrassed about that."

KAZUMI KOBAYASHI (BRACHIOSAURUS):

"We should call it that because that's what Mr. Hammond–all hail The Creator–called it! He gave us life. Besides, Jurassic rules!"

General commotion in the room followed by chant of "Ju-Rass-Ic! Ju-Rass-Ic!" among Jurassic-era dinosaurs. PRESIDENT MARTIN gavels the room to order.

PRESIDENT MARTIN:

"Okay, look. Things are getting heated here and it's late. Some of you want to get back to foraging or eating others of you. I just want a quick show of hands or legs or talons or whatever these appendages I have are [general laughter] to see if any of you have experience in the following areas: accounting [no response], facilities operations [no response], security [no response], advertising [no response], legal?"

PHIL LUNDEEN (DEINONYCHUS) raises his hand.

PRESIDENT MARTIN:

"Wow. Phil. Really? You've done legal work?"

MR. LUNDEEN:

"No, I'm just so hungry right now, Jeff. This is taking forever. I'm wondering if it would be okay to just kill and eat someone here. Someone small like that Compsognathus over there."

MS. KENDRICKS (COMPSOGNATHUS):

"Hey!"

PRESIDENT MARTIN:

"I think this is a good place to stop for now. Good meeting, everyone. We'll meet back here next Thursday and maybe we can do some brainstorming then. No bad ideas. As is customary, we'll ask the predators to remain behind for five minutes to give everyone else a head start."

REJECTED

PROPOSALS

SUPER BOWLS I TO V

SUPER BOWL I—JANUARY 15, 1967

- Folk icon Bob Dylan submitted a proposal to play a set of songs with his guitar plugged into an electric amplifier. The Committee, vomiting with rage, felt that this would be an act tantamount to Judas betraying Jesus Christ, which is certainly not the ideal tone for what it hopes will be an institution.
- John Lennon submitted a proposal to spend the halftime explaining his remarks about being more popular than Jesus. The Committee is of the opinion that this would be kind of a downer. If the Beatles were to perform, that would be one thing but otherwise, no thank you.
- Arizona State University and Grambling State University marching bands were hired instead, along with Al Hirt.

SUPER BOWL II—JANUARY 14, 1968

- Upon receiving the submission for a musical tribute to *The Graduate*, the Committee certainly weighed the possibility. *The Graduate* was the top-grossing film of the last year and it featured a lovely soundtrack by folk duo Simon & Garfunkel. While the Committee feels that the music is perhaps a bit too mellow for a football stadium full of fans, the real problem is the proposed staging. Dustin Hoffman shows no apparent background as a song-and-dance man. Also, the large plate glass window scene would be hard to erect and safely haul away, and the Committee fears that a feeling of directionless American pathos would be difficult to convey at Miami's Orange Bowl.
- Grambling State University's marching band was brought back. Sweet lord how the Committee loves that Grambling band!

SUPER BOWL III—JANUARY 12, 1969

- The Supremes are a well-known and very talented singing group but the Committee was reluctant to accept their proposal to reenact the 1968 election. Leaving aside the obvious dissonance of having a black woman (Flo Ballard) play George Wallace, the Committee simply could not imagine Diana Ross being an effective Richard Nixon.
- Led Zeppelin's "Salute to *Rosemary's Baby*" created similar fears of inexact casting.
- Florida State University's marching band was used, though many Committee members were a little misty-eyed, missing the Grambling band.

SUPER BOWL IV—JANUARY 11, 1970

- Neil Armstrong, Buzz Aldrin, and Michael Collins jointly proposed a panel discussion about the problems they've had readjusting to society. Obviously, the moon landing was the biggest event of the past year and the Committee is very interested in celebrating the achievement. The men's depression is simply not what most Americans choose to think about. The Committee's suggestion to recreate the moon landing as a musical number to the sounds of Sly & the Family Stone was not met with a reply.
- As for the "Woodstock: Super Bowl–style" idea, the Committee feels that the proposed distribution of lysergic acid diethylamide (LSD) to the entire stadium audience is inadvisable due to concerns about legality, health, logistics, and security.
- Carol Channing chosen instead, although she refused to wear a Grambling marching band outfit. Committee made appointment with psychiatrist to deal with Grambling emotions.

SUPER BOWL V—JANUARY 17, 1971

- The Committee received a proposal for Jack Klugman and Tony Randall's salute to the late Jimi Hendrix and Janis Joplin. The Committee understands ABC's desire to promote its new program *The Odd Couple*, but no. Just no. God, no.
- Southwest Missouri State University's marching band was brought in and the Committee was fine, they were just fine.

MUPPET STUDIOS

C A S T I N G O F F I C E

NOTICE OF MUPPETS NOT INVITED TO PARTICIPATE
IN MOVIE AND TELEVISION PROJECTS

August 5, 1976

Hi everyone,

As you know, we will soon be debuting our television show, which we anticipate will be a great success and lead to several major motion pictures. This means new employment opportunities for several of you, including those who weren't really appropriate for *Sesame Street*.

Unfortunately we don't have room for everyone in the cast of this next phase. As always, those of us in the entertainment division will provide stipends to all members of the Muppet species. We know it's hard for you to gain employment given your appearance and the fact that most humans understand you to be puppets made of felt.

So, again, sorry, but here's who's not making the cut and why:

- **Louis the Squirrel.** Too outspoken about anti-Semitic beliefs

- **Mike Rat.** Carries plague

- **Epic Poetry Emu.** We're trying to run a tight show and two-hour poems just don't fit. As a side note, we are still very proud of your MFA.

- **The Amazing Wally.** Chronic explosive diarrhea

- **Geraldine Giraffe.** Too hard to frame in shots; hooked on pain pills

- **Tiny Tom and his Amoeba Troupe.** We never know if they're actually present at any given time. It's possible they may have disappeared, died, or were just imaginary all along.

- **Kevin the Frog.** Kermit feels it is best if his brother is not involved with the show or movies given all that happened as children.

- **Shaggy Pink Monster.** Unlike other big silly monsters, tends to actually kill and eat people

- **Bleedy Bear.** Unable to get insurance

- **The Podiatrist.** Not enough entertainment opportunities for Muppet obsessed with only podiatry

- **Ungrateful Hippo.** Furthers unfortunate (though largely true) stereotype of hippos

- **Muppet God.** Best left as an unseen force rather than physical manifestation

Thanks again, everyone!

J. Henson
Secretary

RESTAURANTS

Cheers
Boston, MA

Ugh! What a disappointment!

The service from our foul-mouthed waitress was terrible and the food didn't even taste like food. Almost like it was just prop food from a play or something? The decor of Cheers is nice enough around most of the place, lots of Boston sports memorabilia but somewhat upscale. But the absolute worst part of Cheers is the spooky abyss of darkness located along one wall. It's not wood, it's not even wall, it's just . . . darkness. We gazed into it for a long time and could have sworn we saw cameras moving around here and there and lighting equipment being adjusted.

Even more eerie is the fact that occasionally a voice will call out from the darkness and the bar staff will suddenly stop everything they're doing and then go back and repeat whatever they had just done! We were so freaked out by that and the dark abyss that we barely noticed the gales of laughter that would occasionally burst forth from nowhere and for no apparent reason.

Regal Beagle

Santa Monica, CA

If there's one thing that characterizes the late 1970s in Southern California, it's an interest in faux English pubs that are haphazardly constructed and operated. Yep, nothing the beach kids and surfers and aspiring starlets crave more than a dark and musty British-themed drinking establishment complete with bartender dressed in oddly formal attire. The Regal Beagle fits that bill! I live right near the place with two girl roommates and, oh, did I mention that I'm a GUY? It's pretty great, but I have to pretend that I'm light in the loafers so that our landlord will allow me to stay there. Here in 1978, landlords are really uptight about that even though we're in California, which is arguably the hedonism capital of the world and supposedly the most open-minded place in America. Anyway, I like to go down to "The Beagle" with my clinically oversexed friend Larry. There's always a table right in front of the camera for us and the other customers never make any sound at all. So yeah, it's pretty great.

What is this magic typewriter I'm using?

Rick's Cafe Americain

Casablanca, Morocco

I'm just going to come out and say it: political tension makes it hard to enjoy your meal! Rick's is a nice enough place, but it is chock FULL of Germans, French resistance operatives on the run, Americans with conflicted allegiances, and Italians of uncertain loyalties. And you never know when things are just going to erupt! I was enjoying my jalapeño poppers appetizer when a group of German officers singing "Die Wacht am Rhein" was drowned out by French sympathizers belting out "La Marseillaise." I mean, HELLO?! I'm trying to enjoy my poppers over here!

Black-and-white decor was neat, though. I don't know how they pulled that off!

Moe's Tavern
Springfield, ?

Dirty, sad, shattered all that I thought I knew about the fundamental tenets of the universe—physics, humanity, and reality due to the oddly animated appearance of the bar and its inhabitants. Pool table was missing equipment.

Soup Kitchen International
New York, NY

★★★★★

This small restaurant has received a great deal of acclaim among those whom Chef deems worthy of eating his soup. That acclaim has led to problems from undesirables in the neighborhood such as marginally successful comedian Jerry Seinfeld and his stupid friend Elaine. They enjoy the soup although they try to mock Chef's authoritative manner by calling him "The Soup Nazi." They are mistaken. Nazis hated Jews and homosexuals. Chef and his followers hate only all foods other than soup.

Seinfeld and his friends don't realize that soup is the master food. It is liquid and solid; it is food and beverage. I am a follower of Chef ever since my early days as a member of Soup Youth. I wear the Soup Party attire to let the world know that I am proud of my meal.

Only when we banish the impure lunch options (pizza, gyros, sandwiches) can we really achieve greatness as diners. If that means invading the Polish restaurant next door or even Monk's Cafe, I'm ready.

Bronto Burgers
Bedrock

⭐⭐⭐

I love the dinosaur ribs. Completely delicious. I just wish they didn't tip over my car every single time I order them. My car is pretty durable, being made of rock and all, but it's still a hassle and the ribs get dirt on them, which is disappointing even for a caveman like me.

HOTELS

Heartbreak Hotel
Lonely Street

★★★

Look, I appreciate theme hotels as much as anyone. I've stayed in tropical hotels. I've stayed in ones decked out to look like the Old West. I even stayed in one decorated like Medieval times! So I was willing to give Heartbreak Hotel a chance.

However, I must report that it just flat BUMMED ME OUT. The whole hotel is based around relationships ending badly! Who thought THAT was a good idea? The bellhop is constantly weeping. The desk clerk is dressed in black and looks like a Marilyn Manson impersonator.

The other guests I talked to at the hotel told me that they were so lonely that they could, in fact, die. How long had they been there? Since their baby left them is all they would say. I was hoping to get some tips on fun places to visit but no dice. The staff and other guests recommended staying in my room and weeping. Hello? What kind of vacation is that?! LOL.

Here's what worries me: if everyone's so lonely they could die, are they really going to die there? Is it more of a Heartbreak Hospice? I don't know. I left in a hurry the next morning.

Two stars because the breakfast buffet was delish! (Skip the pitcher of human tears. Go for the orange juice instead.)

Bates Motel

Fairvale, California

★★★

Pluses: affordable, clean, easy parking.

Minuses: I was stabbed to death in the shower.

Overlook Hotel

Somewhere in Colorado

★★★★

Okay, I want to respond to all the other online reviews I've seen of this place. Sure, several winter caretakers have gone insane there, and, yes, a few of them have killed themselves and their families. If that's a crime, I guess they are guilty.

And if you're easily frightened by creepy ghost twins appearing in the hallways or people in bear costumes giving oral sex to guys in tuxedos, then no, maybe this hotel isn't for you. Go stay at the Super 8, or the Doubletree, or something. But if you like old-fashioned elegance and can put up with the occasional elevator of blood, this is a great place to go.

In the interest of full disclosure, I should point out that I'm a weird ghost butler who hangs out in the bathroom.

Kellerman's Resort

Catskill Mountains, NY

I enjoy dancing but I'm not really crazy about all the "dirty" dancing that goes on here. On the positive side, I found the corners to be refreshingly baby-free.

Sound City Studios

"Home of the Hits"

ENGINEER'S NOTES FROM THE RECORDING OF
FLEETWOOD MAC'S *RUMOURS*

FEBRUARY 4, 1976

All band members arrived today for the start of writing and recording sessions. Immediately, I could tell that this was a band in utter chaos. The success of the previous album was great, but this same success meant pressure that seems to have caused quite a bit of strife. Christine and John McVie are in the process of getting divorced after eight years of marriage. Mick Fleetwood has broken up with his wife after discovering that she was having an affair with his best friend. Lindsey Buckingham and Stevie Nicks, who came into the group as a couple, have mostly split up but seem to have an on-again, off-again thing going on.

The band doesn't speak to each other about any of these personal matters, choosing instead to only talk about the music that they're making. I guess that's a good plan, though I find it hard to believe that they can leave it outside the studio entirely.

Today was mostly setting things up: Stevie's long gauzy scarf collection needed to be inventoried, Lindsey had to find a good place to plug in his curling iron, and a distribution system needed to be found for the remarkable amount of cocaine required by the folk rock musicians of our era.

* * *

FEBRUARY 9, 1976

Lindsey and Stevie broke up and got back together this morning during a demo session for "Never Going Back Again." Pretty sure they might have broken up once more right around the bridge. I couldn't tell for sure because I was too creeped out by the dirty looks Christine was giving John.

* * *

FEBRUARY 11, 1976

There seems to be a detente between Lindsey and Stevie. A workable relationship has been established wherein Lindsey writes and arranges most of the songs and Stevie glares at him while providing harmonies.

More complex is the relationship between the McVies. Their divorce is clearly weighing heavily on Christine who managed to channel it into "Don't Stop," which is a great song that's pretty clearly about someone

(John) struggling with substance abuse and addiction. If you take away the verses and just listen to the chorus, however, you'd think it was a blandly positive feel-good tune, the kind you might use at political rallies or something. Wouldn't that be weird? Say, a presidential candidate using "Don't Stop" to get votes while ignoring that it's really about John McVie's crippling addiction issues?

Anyway, John's playing on the song about his own habits is perfect, but I was embarrassed to learn that John McVie has actually been dead for three days. Yep, massive drug overdose. So who was playing the bass? The cocaine ITSELF. Yep, this is some high-grade shit, capable of keeping a solid bass track rolling along through three days of recording. Good thing Fleetwood Mac is so successful and we could afford the good stuff. Using a defibrillator, some strong coffee, and a shaman that Stevie knew, we got John back and he doesn't seem aware that anything had happened. So it all worked out. We had to pay the cocaine three days of union scale wages. Last I heard, it was hoping to hook up with Foghat.

* * *

FEBRUARY 28, 1976

Stevie is kind of a genius, it turns out. During a break, she found a little room in the back and sat down and wrote a song called "Dreams." It kind of plays out the way she's dealt with her relationship with Lindsey, their breakup, their reuniting, their breakup again, her relationship with the rest of the band, and some other issues that surprised us.

Check out these lyrics from the second verse:

Now here I go again, I see the crystal visions
And by that I mean, of course, cocaine
It's only me who wants to buy a ton more scarves and,
Have you any scarves you'd like to sell?
I'm going to spin around right now,
Like a gypsy witch to drive you mad
In the stillness of remembering I'm Stevie Nicks,
I'm pretty sure I'm Stevie Nicks, am I Stevie Nicks, what kind of name is
    Stevie?
Thunder only happens when it's raining
Look, I'm no expert in climatology
Say, women, they will come and they will go
Could someone make me a scarf made out of cocaine?

They need some tinkering, sure, but I think she's onto something.

* * *

MARCH 9, 1976

Fleetwood Mac has an unlimited budget on this album and really no
constraints of any kind. This means that they roll into the studio at
around 7 p.m. and basically start partying. And because they're such a
hot band, these parties draw plenty of people who have no place in the
creation of music.

Last night alone, we had Sissy Spacek, Marty Feldman, Robert Hegyes, and Ron Palillo from *Welcome Back Kotter*, California Governor Jerry Brown, serial killer Ted Bundy, the 1976 Super Bowl champion Pittsburgh Steelers, Loretta Swit, Lee Majors, and Bigfoot.

Normally I wouldn't mind but after enough drugs and alcohol, a few of these "celebrities" think that playing music isn't all that hard and maybe they could do it too. The band members go along with it and I'm stuck recording all these "sessions" that I know will never make the final cut of *Rumours*.

Among the tracks recorded last night:

- "Revenge of the Lesser Sweathogs"
- "Six Million Dollar Love"
- "I've Got Some Solar Energy Proposals (In My Pants)"
- "You Guys, I Am Seriously a Murderer, This Is Not a Song, It Is a Confession, Please Stop Me"
- "The Steel Curtain of My Cocaine Dreams" (Mean Joe Greene and Stevie duet)
- "Bigfoot Makes Loving Fun"

Again, garbage.

* * *

MARCH 11, 1976

You know what I said about not using those tracks? Yeah, well it turns out Bigfoot is sort of in the band now. At first I didn't notice because I thought it was just Mick in a different outfit. You learn not to question nudity or strong smells around here, but it's Bigfoot alright. He's going out with Christine.

Actually, first it was Christine-Bigfoot, then Stevie-Bigfoot, Lindsey-Bigfoot, Lindsey-Lindsey (thinking it was still Bigfoot), Bigfoot-Mick-Stevie, and back to Christine-Bigfoot. She turned "Bigfoot Makes Loving Fun" into the more vague "You Make Loving Fun." It's not a bad song, actually, and it's good to see her happy.

The tension comes from her insistence that Bigfoot join the band on gong. Very few songs originally had gong in them and it's certainly something that Mick could take care of. But nope, there's Bigfoot, smacking the gong hard at moments no one expects. It's pretty unnerving, especially when you're high as a kite on cocaine. The other band members, of course, complain but Christine sees it as a bold new approach. Everyone's looking to John for guidance on the issue but he's hesitant since he's not sure if Bigfoot is real or if he himself IS Bigfoot.

* * *

MARCH 18, 1976

Bigfoot has left the band. Lindsey lost him to Loggins & Messina in a card game. They'll call themselves Loggins & Messina & Bigfoot now.

*   *   *

MARCH 21, 1976

Final recording sessions are wrapping up. With the suggestion of a label representative, the band has consented to change the titles of several tracks:

- "I'm Dating Someone Else But Still Love Stevie" becomes "Second-Hand News"
- "I Hate Stevie But Love Stevie Who I Hate" becomes "Go Your Own Way"
- "I Painted A Portrait of Bigfoot With My Tears and Eye Shadow" becomes "Songbird"
- "We Keep Fucking One Another!" becomes "The Chain"
- "Mick Resembles a Tree" becomes "Oh Daddy"
- "YAY! I LOVE COCAINE! WHEE!" becomes "Gold Dust Woman"

I'm honored to have worked on this project.

Dear Luke,

Hey Kiddo!

* * *

Dear Luke,

We need to talk. I am your father.

Wow. That sounds so weird to actually say! I have to admit that the role of father is not one that I have dedicated a great deal of time to. I'm sorry.

It's just that work has been so crazy. The kind of particular work I'm involved in is really important, but unfortunately it means that I have to travel A LOT. And I have to kill a lot of

* * *

Whassup Sport!

* * *

Luke,

We've never met but I'm a wealthy moisture baron and would very much like to come visit your moisture farm. It would be strictly to gather information about your moisture farming techniques and not a personal visit because, as I said, we are complete strangers.

There is no ulterior motive to this visit and I would certainly not attempt to lovingly ruffle up your hair, or kill you in a fit of madness/pique, or blow up your planet. Those would be crazy things, after all! Those would be things that a really screwed-up person would do! Like things that someone who sort of accidentally stumbled into a life of evil would do. Not me! NOT ME!

* * *

Luke,

Call me Mr. X. My real identity is not important. I just want to tell you that if you should happen to meet a princess whose hairdo looks like it was inspired by cinnamon rolls, do NOT attempt to make out with her. Trust me. Even if she's attractive in a kind of "cokehead-up-for-anything" kind of way, DON'T GO THERE.

I'll explain later.

Okay fine, I say this because I'm your

* * *

Dearest Luke,

My name is Darth Vader. But it used to be Anakin Skywalker. That's right! Same as your last name! I'm your dad.

I'm telling you this in a letter because I just can't face you after doing what I did. I know, right? Biggest meanest villain in the whole galaxy, but scared to face up to his responsibilities. You see, Luke, being a dad is, well, it's complex. You probably wouldn't understand because you're just a kid, and you're probably really stupid and everything.

I mean, nothing personal. You probably have some potential. You're MY son, after all. And your mom was great. I mean, totally hot. Like, think of the prettiest moisture farm girl that you know, okay? Well, that girl is a filthy hog compared to your mom. In fact, your mom was such a smokin' babe that when I heard she might die, I more or less set out on a series of murders that largely determined the course I am on today. I know, I know, that sounds weird. But Padme . . . you wouldn't believe it. The ass alone. Oh, and she loved you very much and shit like that.

Where was I? Oh yes, you're stupid. Maybe you have potential but I'll have likely blown up your planet before you ever realize it. And I'll have to do that because of reasons.

You see, we have this amazing new secret weapon that we're building. A Death Star! I came up with the name myself. And it can blow up entire planets! Anyone who opposes my employer, really.

Only problem is, the Death Star has one fatal flaw. And I DO mean fatal! There's this little shaft that someone could drop something down and explode the entire thing. Personally, I don't know what's crazier: that we somehow managed to design the thing with that INCREDIBLY DANGEROUS flaw or that we chose to leave it there. I guess it's okay, though, since the only way anyone could find out is if they gained access to a completely unencrypted computer file that's easily copied and distributed. To do that, though, they would need to use one of dozens of free-roaming autonomous droids we have wandering around doing Force knows what.

Anyway, listen to me. I'm talking about myself and my work. How are you, son? Do you play any sports or anything stupid like that?

Mr. Hefti,

First, let me tell you how thrilled we all are to have you on this project. Big fans of your work. We've been playing the demo you sent us and we think the melody you came up with is perfect. Don't change a thing. But we're wondering if you might add some lyrics to it. Audiences may not be familiar with Batman and we think the lyrics could really help people. You don't need to do a whole back story song that we play at the top of every episode, just some kind of introduction to Batman. So you work that up and send it along when you have something.

Sincerely,

Lorenzo Semple, Jr.

Producer

* * *

Who's the
Hero
Who saves
Gotham?
Batman to the rescue
Look out, here comes Batman
Maybe he will rescue you if you are in a pinch
Batman!

* * *

Neal!

Great to see the new lyrics! It's so exciting to work with someone so
talented and creative. I think what I like best about them is how they incor-
porate the name "Batman" three times. It's such a catchy name!

And, of course, it's the name of the TV show that we want people to
remember to watch so the brand awareness is key. I wonder if we might
lean into that a little more, toss a few more mentions of Batman into the
song? And maybe a little more description of who he is?

I want to be clear: I'm not trying to tell you what to do. I'm just
sharing my input as a fellow creative professional, and as the guy who's
developing the series and paying you.

Thanks,
L

* * *

Batman
Caped guy
Batman
Bruce Wayne
Batman is the hero
Hero, name of Batman
Drives a really cool car and Robin is his friend
Batman!

* * *

Neal,

This is progress, my friend. Five mentions of the name "Batman" is better than three! I don't feel like we're quite there yet, however.

Couple of bullet points:

- Let's leave out the mention of Bruce Wayne. We're selling Batman, not the alter ego.
- Same goes for Robin. It's confusing. I don't think there's enough room in the song to explain their complicated relationship, so let's skip it.
- Matter of fact, we don't want to oversell the Batmobile either. Again, I love the song. Such an honor to work with you.

L

Batman
Batman
Super
Hero
Batman to the rescue
Oh good, here comes Batman
He's a superhero and his name is, once again,
Batman!

* * *

Hi Neal,

Okay, I almost feel like this was a step backwards.

- You didn't add any new uses of the name "Batman." Maybe that's my
  fault and I wasn't clear: more. Please.
- Why do you need to keep explaining that he's a superhero? Less
  exposition, more Batman.
- The line second from the end, I feel like it has too many words and they'll
  get all muddled up. Maybe just one word in there? I think you know the
  word I'm talking about! Ha, ha! It's Batman.

Thanks buddy. I know I'm being tough here, but this is important to nail.

Lorenzo

* * *

Batman

Batman

Batman

Batman

Batman Batman Batman

Batman Batman Batman

Batman Batman Batman Batman Batman Batman Batman

Batman!

* * *

Neal,

Wow. What a difference! I know who this song is about now! And I'm not

bogged down by all those other details!

One thing: I'm still having trouble with the second to last line. I almost

feel like we went too far with the Batmans. Which is good! Easier to go too

far and THEN pull back as opposed to not going far enough, right? Any-

hoo, I know you're probably getting impatient with me, but could you put

something in that line that isn't Batman but also isn't any other word?

I guess what I want is NOT Batman and NOT anything else.

Cool? Great. Talk to you soon.

L

* * *

Batman

Batman

Batman

Batman

Batman Batman Batman

Batman Batman Batman

Na na na na na na na na na na na na na

Batman

* * *

Neal!

Perfect! Please find the enclosed check!

You are a brilliant lyricist!

L

REJECTED

PROPOSALS

SUPER BOWLS VI TO X

SUPER BOWL VI—JANUARY 16, 1972

- Another panel discussion proposal: the Nixon administration explains the U.S. approach to the war in Vietnam. It is seen as inappropriate for the festive setting of the Super Bowl, and there are doubts that the scope and complexity of the situation could be adequately explained given the time constraints.
- Tony Randall's salute to the late Jim Morrison is also rejected. Mr. Randall is asked to stop proposing salutes to deceased rock musicians.
- Ella Fitzgerald and Carol Channing (for the second time) booked instead.

SUPER BOWL VII—JANUARY 14, 1973

- *The Godfather* was, by far, the most popular film of the past year but the Committee felt that the proposed halftime salute to the film simply crossed too many lines. The notion of presenting "a more realistic" version of the film included a live execution, the beheading of a horse, and the presence of Marlon Brando, and was therefore regarded to be potentially upsetting to both the stadium crowd and fans watching at home.
- The University of Michigan's marching band seemed like a better idea, so they were hired.

SUPER BOWL VIII—JANUARY 13, 1974

- The Committee received several submissions from the unsuccessful campaign of Democratic presidential nominee George McGovern. After the trouncing by President Nixon in the 1972 election, the remaining staff members felt it would be better to keep Mr. McGovern busy rather than let him dwell on his humiliating defeat. Among the suggestions: selections from McGovern's most cautionary speeches about Vietnam, McGovern's slide show about minimum wage proposals, and a set of Sonny & Cher hits sung with former running mate Thomas Eagleton.
- The Committee was too bummed out for McGovern to fully vet the proposals and chose the University of Texas's marching band instead.

- The Committee is increasingly pessimistic about the viability of Super Bowl musical tributes to popular movies. Several proposals were received this year:

  - *The Towering Inferno.* A three-story building would be assembled on the field, then burned to the ground while Carl Douglas performed "Kung Fu Fighting."

  - *Airport 1975.* Helen Reddy would attempt to land a jumbo jet on the field during halftime. This proposal appeared to be submitted without Ms. Reddy's knowledge or permission. ABBA would perform on the field while hopefully avoiding the airplane.

  - *The Life and Times of Grizzly Adams.* Twenty-five to thirty live bears would be released on the field while actor Dan Haggerty attempted to befriend them. The Steve Miller Band would perform and try to serve as a sort of crew of rodeo clowns, distracting the bears.

- All ideas were rejected. A low-key tribute to Duke Ellington is accepted.

SUPER BOWL X—JANUARY 18, 1976

- The "Getting to know President Ford" proposal meant a difficult decision for the Committee. President Ford believed the nation needed to come together a little more after the recent resignation of President Nixon. While the Committee agreed with that idea, there was less support for the President's specific ideas: interpretive dance to the song "Fox on the Run," the President's impression of comedian Chevy Chase, and his poetic remembrance of McLean Stevenson's Henry Blake character on *M*A*S*H*. It was unclear whether Mr. Ford understood Henry Blake to be a fictional character.

- Concerns over Mr. Ford's capacity to perform such feats without accidentally injuring himself or others led the Committee to green-light the group Up With People instead.

Hi Axl (sic),

Just got your manuscript and demo for the song "Sweet Child o'
Mine."

I think we need to talk.

As your editor, I am responsible for making your songs as cogent
as possible, for helping them reach the high editorial standards your
public has come to expect. With this one, I am certainly earning my
keep. After several attempts to reach you by phone, I am sending
along my notes. Please make appropriate fixes as soon as possible,
at which point I can send them to copyediting and proofreading in
time for your upcoming studio session.

Let's just break these down line by line (and I'll try not to have a
breakdown of my own in the process!)

She's got a smile that, it seems to me—Why equivocate? You
weaken your point by framing this as a mere personal observation
instead of a fact. Are you wasting syllables to fit a rhyme scheme?
Don't do that.

Reminds me of childhood memories—Redundant. You either
have a memory or you're reminded of something. You're not reminded of a memory. Your heavy-metal supporters won't stand for
such writing, my friend.

Where everything was as fresh as a bright blue sky—Okay, I asked around the office and no one is sure a blue sky is necessarily "fresh." You could have a blue sky at the end of a long, sweaty day and there would be nothing fresh about it. And she reminds you of a time when things were fresh? Fond reminiscences of freshness are no foundation for love. Fix.

Now and then when I see her face it takes me away to that special place—Again, you're weakening your own argument. Why does the sight of her face transport you only periodically? And is it just her smile or her entire face that does this to you? Because you've already said both. Consistency, Axel!

And if I stared too long, I'd probably break down and cry—Why would you do that? Because you miss the freshness you described earlier? I think the whole "fresh" thing is really tripping you up. Also, crying? Wimpy. No one likes a whiner.

OK, on to the second verse.

She's got eyes of the bluest skies—See, this is just getting worse. Now her eyes are made of sky? Nice imagery, but you just got done saying her smile reminded you of memories of sky. Is this verse actually supposed to be a second draft of the first verse? Am I confused on formatting? Help!

As if they thought of rain—Axel, hear me now: eyes can't think of rain. And even if they could, which they can't, why would bluest skies think of rain? Perhaps less imagery of thinking eyes made of sky and more direct exploration of your feelings?

I hate to look into those eyes and see an ounce of pain—Well, hell. I guess in your special Axel World anything is possible. Eyes can be made of sky, ponder the weather, and exhibit pain in amounts that can be weighed. I'm sorry to get sarcastic but this is simply awful and it's making me angry.

Her hair reminds me of a warm safe place where as a child I'd hide—Delete. Fix. Do something. You'd hide in a place that reminded you of hair? Never show me such phrases again. I throw up in my brain every time I read that line. And I throw up more each time.

And pray for the thunder and the rain to quietly pass me by— Whew. Okay, listen to me now: Thunder can't quietly do anything. It's thunder. And, more important, do you really want to come across as a wuss who's constantly on the verge of weeping and skittering into hair caves to escape from rain? Is this a song about love or weather anxiety? You need to work these things out.

Finally, Axel, I think we might have had a misunderstanding regarding my previous notes. When I wrote in colored pencil, "Where do we go now?" I wasn't offering that as a lyric. I was simply observing that, in narrative terms, the song needed to progress in some way. You love the girl, she's helping you work through some issues, whatever. So where do we go now? There needs to be an arc in this story.

But instead of providing a satisfactory conclusion, you simply took my note and repeated it over and over again before ultimately just stating the title of the song. This is unacceptable. Don't ask us, the listeners, where we go. That's up to you as the writer! Tell us where we go now!

Again, let's try to fix these things soon and get "Sweet Child of Mine" ("My Sweet Child"?) into your fans' hands as quickly as possible. Because, frankly, if it should ever hit the street in its current form, the song would be a colossal failure.

Talk soon!

Your Editor,
Saul Hudson

Heaven, Guardian Angel Division

Clarence the Angel

**REPORT ON AN ALTERNATE WORLD WHERE
GEORGE BAILEY OF *IT'S A WONDERFUL LIFE* WAS
NEVER BORN, BUT HIS PARENTS RAISED A GRIZZLY
BEAR CUB INSTEAD AND NAMED IT GEORGE**

Dear God,

I have recently completed George Bailey's tour of another version of his life wherein he had never been born. In this latest one, we posited that Ma and Pa Bailey had found an orphaned bear cub in the woods, born the same day as George was in the dominant reality, and raised it as a son named George.

As one might expect, it is not a pretty picture. As always happens, it certainly doesn't turn out nearly as well as the one wherein human George Bailey is born.

In this scenario, Harry Bailey falls through the ice and is not pulled to safety. But rather than simply drown, he is severely mauled by his "brother" George and then his shredded corpse tumbles beneath the ice. Horrifying.

Again, as in most scenarios presented to human George, the affordable housing development known as "Bailey Park" never gets built. Ma and Pa were coping with the tragedy of losing Harry while raising a dangerous bear in their home. Therefore, they were not well positioned to make much of a splash in either the banking or real estate industries. Mostly they just cowered and wept.

Of course, grizzly George never falls in love with Mary Hatch. In fact, the big high school dance where Mary and human George were to fall into the swimming pool, sealing their love, was the scene of a savage display of a grizzly's mercurial nature. Grizzly George, mistakenly thinking there are salmon in the gymnasium, shows up at the dance, gets very agitated at all the music and commotion, and responds in the way a grizzly bear naturally would. One can't really blame him for being what, well, You made him. But at the same time, one can't really feel good about the bloodbath in the gym.

Again, Mary works at the library, which serves as a sort of emergency shelter where people can run when George is on the loose and hungry.

Come to think of it, the whole grizzly George alternate universe mostly serves as a scathing indictment of Ma and Pa Bailey's horrible judgment and the criminally negligent practices of the Bedford Falls animal control department.

George, the bear, does take up with Violet Bick for a furtive romance that ends with each getting very hurt, although in extremely different ways.

Grizzly George does manage to maul Mr. Potter to death, forestalling the development of Pottersville, so at least there's that. That doesn't really save the town, mind You, because people are still terrified to go outside much. Eventually the town is abandoned except for the deeply insane Ma and Pa Bailey and their bear son.

Not a happy ending.

But, Lord, none of them are happy endings. None of the dozens of alternate George Bailey lives I have shown him end up being very positive. And I believe we established that in the first and—I think—most elegant parable we showed him: if he had simply never been born. After that, George treasured his life, appreciated his blessings, and things turned out great! I got my wings (thanks) and that seemed to be the end of it. But it wasn't. You sent me back to "help" George some more. Your ways, Lord, are well-established to be mysterious. So I'm going with it, but I'd like the record to show that I am confused and dubious.

Still, when I got the instructions to show him a world where he had been born, left in the jungle, raised by wolves, and returned at age 18, I obliged. As we know, that was not a positive world either. In subsequent months, I was asked to show him yet more worlds:

- George is born, but he's a robot.

- George is born and he's just the same, but everyone else in town is a vampire.

- George is born and he's just the same, but everyone else in town is a porcupine.

- Mary is a killbot sent from the future to eliminate George before he can ever build Bailey Park.

- George and all the characters are in an airplane that explodes in mid-air and they land on an island that becomes Bedford Falls.

I'm pretty sure You got that last one from the TV show *Lost*.

The construction of alternate realities is very time-intensive for angels and I'm getting complaints. This has also become really time-consuming for the real George, whom I have to rouse from bed three or four times a week. He's awfully sore about that and it's having a pretty negative effect on his family, which seems counterproductive.

I beg You to move off the constant haranguing of George Bailey. I need to get working on that stupid movie with Nicolas Cage and Meg Ryan that's all about angels. I know it's a remake of the Wim Wenders' movie, but the German angels are working on that.

Thanks,

Clarence

Rod Serling Productions

TO: PRODUCTION TEAM, STAFF WRITERS
FROM: SERLING
RE: REJECTED *TWILIGHT ZONE* EPISODE IDEAS

Thank you for all your hard work in coming up with ideas. The following is a list of pitches we will not be using in the coming season. I hope to never see these ideas again, in fact. I wish I had never seen them.

Rod

"Here Come Aliens." Setting: a sleepy town in the Midwest where everyone is going about their business. The local lunatic insists that aliens are about to invade and destroy everything. "Nothing will be the same once the aliens get here!" he insists. Everyone writes it off as mad ramblings until a local farmer hires some Mexicans to pick his berry crop. Before long, there are Mexicans all over the place, taking our jobs and living off government handouts. I mean, there was a time when people who belonged here would do those jobs. Meanwhile, the goddamn liberal government doesn't do anything about it. All they care about is tax and spend, tax and spend. Bunch of heads-up-their-ass politicians. Where's the fucking remote? IT'S IN THE TWILIGHT ZONE.

"A Date with Death." A self-centered and vain woman goes on a blind date, agreeing to meet a gentleman at a restaurant. When she arrives for their date, he is wearing a cloak over his head and introduces himself as Death. She realizes that she has actually died! He agrees to return her to the world of the living if she does one good deed for someone else. She offers to do some volunteer work at a homeless shelter, but Death says that she needs to sleep with that guy Jeff who works in accounting at her office. At that point, she realizes that "Death" is really Jeff in disguise. But when she pulls the cloak from his head, it's a skull teeming with worms! It really was Death! Turns out Death and Jeff had set the whole thing up, though, because Death is super into watching people do it. Death gets thrown out of the restaurant. Cut to Jeff furiously masturbating IN THE TWILIGHT ZONE.

"The Mouse That Kills People." What about a mouse that kills people? I don't know. I'll need to flesh this one out a little. But wouldn't that be weird? A mouse? Whoa. TWILIGHT ZONE!

"What's Going On with This Space Mission?" Three astronauts set off to land on the moon but then a blast of space radiation sends them off course. They pass out but wake up to find themselves landing. They assume it's the moon, but the terrain is different. It looks a lot like the desert in California. Then there's a rabbit or something, so they're sure they landed back on Earth. But the rabbit has a space helmet on! So maybe it's the moon! But THEN! Some guy comes up to them and he's all green and wearing a silver jumpsuit, so it must be some different planet. One of the astronauts takes off his helmet and the other astronaut realizes that the first astronaut is his father! Whoa! So did they go back in time or something? Then the third astronaut is Ben Franklin! And the whole thing is happening in a warehouse. A warehouse IN THE TWILIGHT ZONE. Weird, right?

"Atomic War Hooray." We open just as the missiles are hitting targets and mushroom clouds are erupting all over the world. Yes, millions of people die but everyone agrees that things were getting awfully crowded around the planet anyway. Lots of animals and plants are wiped out and all the lakes and rivers are poisoned. This takes away many sources of food for the surviving humans but guess what: the radiation makes all the humans into superhumans who no longer need food and water. Everyone is ten feet tall and super athletic and good looking and smart. And they have sex all over the place. Now I know that this is where the twist comes in and something ironic happens when people realize that maybe this isn't heaven at all but a form of hell. Like maybe they only live for five minutes or something. But the twist here is: there is no twist. Life is just super awesome forever. This pitch co-sponsored by Boeing and General Electric. Headquartered IN THE TWILIGHT ZONE.

"The Raffle Ticket." A couple buys a raffle ticket at a carnival. They end up winning the grand prize of an all-expenses-paid, two-week vacation. They are delighted to receive this news but fail to note where the vacation will take place: Barf Island. Yep, the island where everyone barfs all the time. Okay, the twist: they really like it and end up buying and running their own resort there and live there, constantly barfing. You can send away for a brochure IN CARE OF THE TWILIGHT ZONE. Note: it would be really great if you could get Doris Day and Rock Hudson to star in this one.

"The Thief's Assistant." A bank robber's big heist goes wrong when a security guard, in an attempt to stop the robbery, shoots himself to death. The ghost of the guard follows the robber to his hideout, not aware that he is dead. The robber, not really a bad guy at heart, relays the bad news to the guard and eventually takes him on as an assistant for a series of burglaries. It's a sweet setup: ghost frightens the homeowner out of the house, robber grabs the loot. Over the years, their friendship grows stronger and they leave the life of crime and open a small bed and breakfast. Years go by and nothing much happens. The former robber dies but produces no ghost. The ghost is sad forever because his soul cannot be transported. Their divergent paths reveal that life ultimately leads to death, which will either be nothingness or isolation. And are those things really that different after all? I mean, if you're alone and out of contact with anyone, isn't it just the same as the cessation of being itself? Maybe there's a pie fight at the end or something IN THE TWILIGHT ZONE.

Please find enclosed the complete British Intelligence files on the fates of Agents 001 through 006. These files are for your eyes only, only for you.

—M

AGENT 001—ALBERT FROST. STATUS: DECEASED

Mr. Frost was the first agent in the history of British intelligence to receive a designated agent number. Being well-regarded within our operation, he was assigned the number 001, the two zeros being placed there with some degree of hope that we would receive funding to hire hundreds more, a wish that remains unfulfilled.

Mr. Frost was deployed to stop international jewel thief Silas Query, aka Dr. Query, or sometimes the unpronounceable "?". Having stolen valuable items from several major museums, Query had set his sights on the Crown Jewels of England.

According to guards nearby, Frost had cornered Query in an entryway of Buckingham Palace. Agent 001 looked at Query with a bemused expression and said, "Well, Dr. Query. The only question now seems to be whether you will perish here or be sent to prison." Then Dr. Query shot Frost to death.

The lesson learned from the death of Agent 001 is that bons mots are not enough in apprehending a criminal. An agent must either display a credible threat to the suspect or have the ability to get out of a dangerous situation. After Frost's passing, the agency chose to start arming agents. It was seen as somewhat shameful that this had not been considered in advance.

AGENT 002—LIAM WINCHESTER. STATUS: DECEASED

Mr. Liam Winchester, unlike his predecessor, carried a handgun. His undoing, however, was the combination of that weapon and Winchester's penchant for alcohol. Whilst undercover at a Monte Carlo casino, on the trail of an international art thief, Winchester ordered a Martini. The drink was brought to him shaken although he preferred his Martinis stirred.

Not being well trained in the appropriate use of handguns, Agent 002 drew his weapon and used it to stir his Martini. Various criminals spotted the gun, sussed out that Winchester was a law enforcement agent, and swiftly killed him.

From the death of Agent 002, we learned that one should be discreet about one's weapon. Also, to be on the safe side, agents should henceforth order Martinis shaken and not stirred. One might go so far as requesting agents not to drink on the job at all, but seeing as how we employ only the most desperate and self-destructive of alcoholics, this is not seen as an attainable goal.

AGENT 003—LEONARD DUNN. STATUS: MISSING

After Winchester's death, there was an emphasis placed on discipline among the agents. Yes, they were allowed to have cocktails (one must drink, after all), but otherwise the job was to be all business. This included one's social life whilst on assignment. To wit, no dating and certainly no sex.

Mr. Dunn, prior to this rule, quite fancied the ladies and was known to frequently be seen with a beautiful girl on his arm. His loyalty to country and Queen was stronger, however, and he dutifully abided by the rules. For a while.

Ultimately, his need for sex and his sense of responsibility collided with such violent force that his brain snapped. Agent 003 was last seen wandering the streets of London taping Union Jacks over the breasts of women in fashion adverts.

AGENT 004—A GOAT. STATUS: DECEASED

This particular approach was doomed from the start. We'll leave it at that.

AGENT 005—NIGEL TEMPLETON. STATUS: RESIGNED IN DISGRACE

With the hiring of Mr. Templeton, we initiated a complete overhaul of our approach to the agents.

OUT:
- Celibacy
- Goats (obviously)

IN:
- Highly advanced weaponry (can't rely on one gun in a world rapidly becoming more dangerous).
- Clever minds capable of witty repartee, so much the better to banter with baddies and seduce women who might be able to share valuable information.
- Fucking.

Mr. Templeton was named Agent 005 and was put on the trail of a menacing organized crime kingpin. This assignment required Agent 005 to maneuver through the highest social circles of the French Riviera. His progress was somewhat limited, however, by the attire he had been assigned. Templeton was given a pair of denim overalls with large patches in gaudy fabric on them, and with the strap on one shoulder broken. He was also given a comically large straw hat and a corncob pipe. We gave Agent 005 no shoes and encouraged him to walk around barefoot.

Details are still somewhat sketchy on the exact rationale behind such a wardrobe assignment. Inspectors found a single memo saying, "Everybody LOVES hillbillies!" and that seems to be about all the thinking that went into it.

Obviously, such a disguise was not effective among the glitterati and hill-billies are not a native concept to the British. Agent 005 failed and hundreds of people died as a result. Templeton resigned. Last we heard, he was running moonshine stills in America.

After this disaster, a more stringent dress code was implemented. Posh fashions only.

AGENT 006—CLIVE EDWARDS. STATUS: DECEASED

Mr. Edwards, we were convinced, had it all going for him: a knowledge of weaponry, sharp clothes, quick wit, alcoholism, a way with women. He was the perfect spy.

So confident were we that when he was captured by hyperintelligent mad-man Dr. Cruelty, we were sure that he would escape. Dr. Cruelty, true to his name, strapped Agent 006 to a conveyor belt that moved ever-so-slowly to-ward a highly charged laser beam that would slice right through Agent 006, killing him. Dr. Cruelty then left the room, confident that the laser would kill Agent 006.

Which it did. The photos are quite gruesome.

It was a difficult time for the agency and the British government as a whole. What more could we do to protect our agents when they were all, ulti-mately, human and thus fallible?

"What if," M asked, "we didn't rely on just one person?"

Here was a true turning point. In the construction of Agent 007, we opted to rotate the role through various people. We could start with, say, a good-looking macho Scotsman, then if we get tired of him or he wants too much money or he feels that his range is being limited by being associated with the Agent 007 role, we just move on. Maybe give the job to a more droll Brit, then a couple of guys no one liked all that much, and then a blond guy who everyone thinks is pretty hot.

With this approach, we believe Agent 007 can, in effect, live forever.

TOP SECRET

BLINKY, Red Ghost · · · · · · · · · · · · · · · · ·

> I think it's easy for someone to come in
> here and say, "Wow, you live in a maze,
> that must be terrible." To me, living in
> a big house with huge rooms, that would
> be terrible. In the maze, there's always
> somewhere to hide. When we were kids it was
> a blast. Epic hide-and-seek games. Epic.
> And now as ghosts, hiding is just kind of a
> natural inclination for us. I'm happy here.

PINKY, Pink Ghost · · · · · · · · · · · · · · · · ·

> We haven't let death interfere with the
> operation of the farm. No, sir.

INKY, Cyan Ghost · · · · · · · · · · · · · · · · ·

> All four of us siblings, we've always been
> very close. We grew up together here in the
> maze. Our parent ran the pellet farm, just
> as his parent had before. We kind of all
> refer to him as a him, but in truth we are
> genderless. I have never known genitalia.

CLYDE, Orange Ghost · · · · · · · · · · · · · · · ·

> Dad somehow generated us from his own body.
> We don't know how he did that.

PINKY . . . .

A lot of people wonder, "Oh, was it Pac-Man
who killed your father?" But it wasn't. It
was pancreatic cancer. It took many years
and it was incredibly painful.

BLINKY . . . .

In the last few months it was particularly
difficult for all of us because of, you
know, the maze that we live in. We'd
hear him call out for pain medicine or
something, glass of water, and all four of
us would zip around trying to figure out
where he was this time. But he refused to
be moved to hospice care. The pellet farm
mattered that much to him.

INKY . . . .

So when he died, the four of us kept
running the farm. We weren't suited for any
other kind of work.

BLINKY . . . .

The outside world can always use a good
crop of nutrient pellets. And the money we
made from that could get us what we needed
to get by: security for the maze, routine
maintenance, fruit to eat. We'd plant a new
pellet crop and then keep going.

CLYDE . . . .

I dreamed of getting out of here. I'll be
honest. I was . . . am . . . kind of the
rebel of the group. Look at my name. I
was interested in moving to Portland and
maybe opening a coffee shop. I thought
getting into social work would have been
interesting; go back to school for that if
necessary.

INKY . . . .

Clyde was ridiculous. Family is family and
our family is pellet farmers.

CLYDE . . . .

So I stayed. And I'm still here.

INKY . . . .

Blinky has always kind of run things. Clyde
certainly couldn't do it, so distracted.
Pinky and I, we're followers.

BLINKY . . . .

We had a good life. We got by. Dying was
unfortunate. I did not see death coming.

PINKY . . . .

Gas leak. We were all asleep and we just
never woke up.

INKY . . . .

It actually took us most of that morning
to realize that we had become ghosts. We
sat down to breakfast but, after a while,
realized that the fruit we were eating was
still on the plate. We checked in our room,
the only room, the one in the middle of the
maze, and our bodies were there.

BLINKY . . . .

So we burned them and got right back to
work.

CLYDE . . . .

It was a hard day for me. If death wasn't
going to get me out of here, what good
would all these grad school applications do
me?

INKY . . . .

Things continued like that for, gosh,
I don't know how long. I mean, I really
don't. You tend to lose track of time when
you're dead.

PINKY . . . .

Sometimes Clyde and I would run into each
other in the upper-right quadrant or
something and talk about why we were still
here. Like, is there unfinished business or
something? Why haven't we moved on to the
next plane, you know?

CLYDE . . . .

We tried to bring that up to Blinky once.

BLINKY . . . .

We are here to farm the pellets. It's a
stupid question and it's a waste of time.

INKY . . . .

I'll never forget when I heard that
horrible sound for the first time. Wocka.
Wocka.

PINKY . . . .

Wocka wocka wocka.

CLYDE . . . .

Wocka wocka wocka wocka wocka wocka wocka
wocka wocka wocka.

PINKY ·

Then I saw this horrible color, this . . .
yellow. This thing was all mouth. Literally
all mouth.

BLINKY ·

First, I thought, "What the FUCK does this
guy think he's doing?" Then I thought,
"Destroy." Instinct kicked in.

CLYDE ·

Someone must have left a door open or
something. But it doesn't have hands.
How did it get here? Anyway, we were all
with Blinky on this. Get it. Kill that
motherfucker.

INKY ·

Thing is, wherever it goes, it eats
pellets. It's not like we have a farm
house and then fields out back. We're not
oat farmers. We're not cattle ranchers.
We raise nutrient pellets. The only place
pellets can grow is inside a maze. Everyone
knows that. So the more we chase it, the
more it consumes.

BLINKY ·

I remember the first time we caught it,
we were so happy. We thought it was just a
freak occurrence that had been taken care
of. But then it showed up again. So we
killed it again. And then it came back once
more! After that killing, we had peace for
a while.

CLYDE ·

It seems to always get three lives at a
time.

PINKY ·

The big pellets were my idea. I thought it
could be really great for business. Maybe
people would pay more and then we could
have fruit all the time, you know? I spent
a lot of time genetically engineering these
things.

INKY ·

Look, I happen to believe in a larger plan.
Pinky defiled nature and now we must all
pay the price. We were all swayed at first.
The big pellets were attractive. But the
devil is in the details and the details in
this case were disastrous for us.

CLYDE . . . .

The first time Pac-Man ate one of the big
pellets, I can't even describe the feeling.
It was like being hollowed out. Like you
know in Harry Potter when the Dementors
attack Harry and he feels like all hope is
gone? We turned blue.

PINKY . . . .

One time, back when I was alive, I went
off my meds for a few days. The big pellets
being eaten feels like that times ten.

BLINKY . . . .

I never expected to shut down like that.
And Pac-Man senses that and just attacks.

CLYDE . . . .

When Pac-Man first ate me, I thought,
well, okay. Now I get out. Now I move on to
heaven or hell or nothing. And so there was
a sense of relief, almost.

INKY . . . .

But then we come back as ghosts in that
room again. Still dead, but powerful once
more.

PINKY . . . .

How many forms can death take?

BLINKY . . . .

I love it. I LOVE being reborn as a ghost
because it's a chance to go after that
fucker again.

INKY . . . .

Blinky knows what's best. We all trust him.

CLYDE . . . .

The emergence of Pac-Man has really made
me think about things a lot. Like why do
we maintain the farm at all? We raised the
pellets to sell the pellets, right? So we
could have money to buy fruit. Which we can
no longer eat.

INKY . . . .

It's nice to have the fruit around. I wish
we could eat that fruit.

PINKY . . . .

Pac-Man is the only who eats the fruit
anymore. Blinky and Inky set it out
as, I don't know, some kind of totem of

the living, some kind of effort toward
normalcy. But really, it's just a sacrifice
to Pac-Man.

CLYDE . . . .

I think we love Pac-Man. I would go a step
further. I think we worship Pac-Man. Pac-
Man gives our life meaning. We chase him,
we destroy him, or we are destroyed by him.
But no matter what happens, there is always
rebirth.

PINKY . . . .

I would like to die. Really die. I don't
think I ever will.

INKY . . . .

Sometimes I gaze out into space, which is
easy to do because the maze has no roof.
And I think I see people walking toward me.

PINKY . . . .

I do believe in the sky people. I do. Maybe
I'm crazy but just before Pac-Man arrives,
I think I see them.

CLYDE . . . .

I don't talk about religion much with
Blinky. I don't want to get him or her, it,
Blinky, I don't want to get Blinky upset.
But I think the sky people bring us Pac-
Man. I think that explains what Pinky and
Inky see, I think that explains the sound
of something being dropped down a slot. I
think it's all part of the plan. The sky
people are God and they send us their only
son, Pac-Man.

BLINKY . . . .

Pellets.

INKY . . . .

Blink.

CLYDE . . . .

God.

PINKY . . . .

Death.

Ozzy,

I was looking at the lyrics of "War Pigs":

> *Generals gathered in their masses*
> *Just like witches at black masses*

Do you realize you rhymed "masses" with "masses"?

Tony

* * *

Tonq,

Greezuh humfit du lowrind. Whavuh clem? Sorssin rockyroll.

Ozzuh

* * *

Ozzy,

Very well. Carry on.

Tony

THE BAR

Hi Mr. Joel,

It's been awfully hard to find time to talk at the club since I'm busy managing the place and you're at the piano. Doing your thing. I've occasionally given you a nervous smile hoping it would initiate a conversation, but that hasn't worked out. I'm hoping that by writing my thoughts down, you'll have a chance to read this when you're at home or something.

I'll come right out with it: I need you to sing songs. Actual songs. Because you don't sing any at all right now. You've been playing at my club for three months, and though you're a fine musician and an acceptable vocalist, these things you perform are simply not songs in the traditional sense. They're streams of observations about what the people in the club are doing right at that exact moment, punctuated by the occasional "la la la, de de da" when it's clear you've run out of things to say. It's a continuous stream of musical small talk lasting up to five hours. How about "Stormy Weather" or "Yesterday" or something? Hell, "Feelings." Anything.

Do you need sheet music? I have some at home. I can bring it in. Do you even know how to play songs?

Frankly, this has been bothering me since you started, but I figured since we get a regular crowd shuffling in on Saturdays when you play, why rock the boat? This past Saturday, however, I couldn't help notice that there was a lot of tension in the room. As you know, it was a pretty good crowd that night, customers who wanted to forget about life for a while by having some drinks and hearing some music. John, the bartender, provided the booze, as always, so they looked to you for the songs.

Of course, I don't need to tell you that. You put what he did in the song, too. You had to be a big shot, didn't you? Billy, that kind of thing is why people kept yelling at you all night. "Sing us a song, piano man! Sing us a SONG tonight!" they shouted. But instead of doing so, you simply shouted their words back to them and added a line about how you were making them feel all right. Which you weren't. You were making them mad. People aren't just in the mood for a melody, they're in the mood for a legitimate composition with a competent arrangement. Are you stupid, Billy Joel?

They were annoyed, too, because the observations were as cruel as they were specific. Davy often discusses his plans for when he gets out of the Navy (it's a steady paycheck although the rhyming-name thing annoys the hell out of him), but to hear you speculate that he would be there for life was a crushing blow. No one likes to think of himself as being at a dead end. Again, why the public humiliation? And our businessmen were irate about your description of them getting "stoned." Do you not know the difference between drunk and stoned? Hint: One is acceptable businessman behavior, the other is illegal.

Even if you were to say they were getting drunk, that still would not be okay. As a matter of fact, just don't sing about the business-men. They're nice guys and good tippers.

I guess I do owe you some thanks, however, for singing about the drink called "Loneliness." That's a terrible name for a drink. I'm renaming it "Banana Mambo." More festive.

As to our waitress's efforts to get a graduate degree in political science or Paul's attempt at pioneering the literary genre of real-estate fiction, Jesus, Billy, leave them alone.

So for next week: Please sing some actual songs. That's what you were hired to do. You're the fucking piano man.

Thanks,

Anthony Cacciatore
Manager

REJECTED

SUPER BOWL HALFTIME SHOW

PROPOSALS

SUPER BOWLS XI TO XV

SUPER BOWL XI—JANUARY 9, 1977

- A notable proposal called for The Sex Pistols, purveyors of "punk rock" to perform, although the Committee was unclear whether the group would play music, refuse to play music, inject themselves with heroin, or simply assault the crowd at the Rose Bowl in Pasadena. The Committee was more positive about the proposed finale of the act, which would involve young actor Sylvester Stallone, star of *Rocky*, to run on the field and beat members of The Sex Pistols into unconsciousness.
- Scheduling conflicts arose, however, and the spot was ultimately given to the Los Angeles Unified All-City Band. Because people love marching bands!
- Carol Channing's offer to return for a third appearance was politely declined.

SUPER BOWL XII—JANUARY 15, 1978

- The rock group known as the Eagles submitted a proposal to perform a medley of their hit songs in a show that would involve fairly large and complicated set pieces, including:
  - A corner in Winslow, Arizona, and a flatbed Ford
  - Fences and a Desperado to ride upon them
  - A "cheatin' side of town" (perhaps the end zone?)
- A counteroffer to the group was made wherein they would simply play the songs. This offer was declined.
- Tony Randall showed up dressed as the deceased Elvis Presley, but was rebuffed at the gate.
- A college drill team was brought in along with Al Hirt. The Committee loves Al Hirt. Nothing says football like Al "Mr. Super Bowl" Hirt.

SUPER BOWL XIII—JANUARY 21, 1979

- The "Disco Forever" proposal held a lot of promise. People like music and people like dancing, so there was some potential there. Where the Committee felt the proposal crossed a line was the idea of converting the Miami Orange Bowl into a replica of Studio 54, complete with Bianca Jagger riding a white horse, 5,000 Truman Capotes gossiping with 5,000 Andy Warhols, and an ounce of cocaine (with silver spoon) to be placed under each audience member's seat. The Committee was confident that a more practical disco tribute could be produced in years to come when disco would still be popular and relevant.
- Caribbean bands hired. Why the hell not?

SUPER BOWL XIV—JANUARY 20, 1980

- The overwhelming box office success of the divorce film *Kramer vs. Kramer* and the producers' desire to appeal to Oscar voters led to a proposal for a *Kramer vs. Kramer* halftime show. The idea was quite simple. All fans seated on the western side of the Rose Bowl would be given latex masks of Meryl Streep. Fans on the eastern side would receive latex masks of Dustin Hoffman. At halftime, all fans would don their masks and child actor Justin Henry would walk, completely alone, to the center of an empty football field. Then the fans would have to yell their best arguments as to why Justin Henry should come and sit with them. Whoever makes the best arguments wins. The Committee feared a weepy crowd would be unable to enjoy the game.

- A preemptive note was sent to Tony Randall advising him against any potential tribute to the late John Wayne or Zeppo Marx.

- The Committee, unable to really break with the past, brought back the Grambling State University marching band for one more game. No regrets.

SUPER BOWL XV—JANUARY 25, 1981

- The Committee was happy to learn that the administration of newly elected President Ronald Reagan was interested in creating a halftime show, but found the ideas to be difficult to execute:

  - The Trickle Down Cascade effect, wherein millions of dollars would be released from the top of the Superdome to "trickle down" to fans below, was tested. Results of the test indicated that the money would be simply grabbed by the people who got to it first.

- The administration's idea of giving each fan a large bottle rocket to simulate the upcoming arms buildup also seemed dangerous, especially in a domed stadium. The administration pointed out that with everyone armed, there was actually less of a chance of anyone lighting off a bottle rocket, but that made no sense.

- Also, the American hostages recently released in Iran were not interested in reenacting their own capture while Lionel Richie and Barbra Streisand sang.

- Committee just hired the Southern University marching band instead.

From: Commander
To: All Crew

....

Comrades,

I'm afraid I have to confirm the speculation that
has been going around the ship. In our hasty
departure from Earth, it appears we have left one
of our number behind. The crew member known as
Eetay is presently not accounted for and we are
left to assume that he is still on the surface of
the planet. He must have wandered too far from the
craft while gathering samples of the native flora
and not returned in time.

In addition to returning the ship to the planet
to rescue Eetay, we will immediately begin a re-
evaluation of our departure procedures to ensure
that this does not happen again.

Be vigilant.

From: First Mate
To: Commander, All Crew

....

Obviously, the error here is a serious one.
Like all crew members, I wish that this had not
occurred.

However, I invite you to consider whose fault this
truly was. Everyone else made it back to the ship
in plenty of time. Being on this ship means having
certain duties and responsibilities and Eetay
failed to meet those responsibilities.

From: Commander
To: First Mate, All Crew

....

Um . . . Okay. So what's your point, Dan?

From: First Mate
To: Commander, All Crew

....

It's going to cost a great deal of fuel to return
to Earth, land the craft, locate Eetay, and
rescue him. It's also very dangerous since, as we
understand from Earth's TV transmissions, everyone

101

has a gun and most of them are stupid. Given that
this is a crewman lacking in common sense and that
he's not likely to prove to be all that valuable
a crew member in the future, shouldn't we at least
consider, you know, leaving him there? Chalking it
up to an acceptable loss, in business terms?

From: Commander
To: First Mate, All Crew

....

Absolutely not! I'm really surprised that you would
even suggest this. We don't leave people behind,
even the most inept crew members. Please set a
course for Earth at once.

From: Crew member #641
To: All

....

I gotta say, I kind of agree with Dan. I have never
liked that dude. I worked with him on the crystal
fuel ports for a while and he just talked weird.
Like, I would be talking about my family, sports,
whatever. And talking like a normal person. But
then Eetay would talk in this weird slow way, like,
"Fuuuuuuellll Pooooorts." And I'm all, "Yeah, have
you heard anything I've been talking about?"

From: Crew member #344
To: All

....

Did he ever get empathic with you guys? He did it
to me once, WHILE I WAS SLEEPING, MIND YOU. And
then I had this weird link to him where we felt the
same things and I understood the loneliness and
despair in his heart. It was awful. God, I hate
that dude.

From: Crew member #819
To: All

....

And have you noticed that when he tries to heal
something with his finger, it glows all red? What's
up with that? What a freak!

From: Commander
To: All

....

Are we really going to go there? Do I need to send
everyone back to diversity and sensitivity training
again? Just because we don't have anyone from HR on
this particular ship doesn't mean we don't have to
follow all the policies set forth in the Employee

Handbook. The fact remains that Eetay is one of us
and we take care of our own.

From: First Mate
To: All

....

Commander, I totally respect your point of view.
And you are the commander so what you say goes.

From: Commander
To: All

....

Thank you. Full speed ahead.

From: First Mate
To: All

....

It's just . . . I want to make sure you recognize
that this might be a kind of opportunity. Eetay is
freaky looking. Remember when we landed on that one
planet and there were all these local girls there
and things were going reeeeeeally well between us

and them and they were super cute? But then Eetay
shows up. He's naked. He's all wrinkly looking.
He's moving his weird long neck up and down. And
then before you knew it, boom, the babes all had to
"get up early in the morning." Dude totally ruined
it for us!

From: Commander
To: All

....

I do remember that night. That was awful.

Look, if we do this, and it looks like everyone
wants it to happen, we need to make sure we all
keep the same story.

So: He was eaten by a bear. Okay? That's what we
say to everyone. We send back pictures of a bear.
People will totally buy it.

I think he lived alone in a small apartment. I
doubt he'll be missed.

From: First Mate
To: All

....

Oh crap. He's calling. I can see the caller ID on
the phone. How did he even get our number?

From: Commander
To: All

....

To Earth, then. Please delete all e-mails on this
subject. Shit.

From the Desk of The Power

Easy Street, America

July 4, 2005

Dear Chuckdee, Flavor Flavor,
Professor Griffin, and everyone else,

Hey, guys! What's up? Or should I say "what up"? Is that how you hippity-hoppers and homeyboys and gangerbangers are saying it now? Never mind. I'll get right to the point.

Do we have to keep fighting like this? Or, more specifically, do you really want to keep fighting me? I don't mind indulging you if that's what you guys want. It's not hurting me, of course, since I am The Power. But I just wonder if you might consider giving it up. I mean, this has been going on for a while and I'm still very much here.

Do you realize that you've been fighting me since 1989? Now, that's sixteen years ago. Babies born that summer are grown-ups now! So much has happened since then. Presidents have come and gone, the Soviet Union collapsed. But not The Power! Honestly, guys, I'd really like to be your friend and hang out with you at your rapping concerts. It's time to put this behind us.

And I wonder if I might offer you some constructive criticism. Among the problems, I think, has been your clarity of precisely why you were fighting me and how you intended to wage that fight. Like when you say: "As the rhythm designed to bounce / What counts is that the rhymes / Designed to fill your mind."

Pardon my frankness but what the hell are you talking about there? It rhymes, but what are people supposed to do with that information? If you're trying to fight someone, especially someone like me, you need clear action items. Maybe "Carjack The Power's limousine after an important board meeting," or "Expose The Power's malfeasance in a national publication," or maybe "Propose a better alternative to The Power and let the people decide." Those are just off the top of my head! Look, take this advice or don't, but before dismissing it just remember The Power must know what he's doing, right? Thus the name. Think about it.

Let's take a look at your other complaints. You don't care for Elvis Presley. That's fine. I would encourage you to rewatch the '68 comeback special, but whatever. And say what you want about Elvis (was he really a straight-up racist? I didn't know that!), but he's certainly not part of The Power. By the way, I agree with you on John Wayne. I've never seen the appeal. Where was the range? So we don't really have a quarrel there, do we?

And what do you have against Bobby McFerrin? Yes, "Don't Worry, Be Happy" was the No. 1 "jam," but honestly, it's a really great song—the things that man does just with his voice are amazing. A lot of people found it fresh and innovative and not all Grumpy Gus like some people's music (hint hint! ha ha, just kidding, but I have a point). The success of Bobby's song had nothing to do with me. I'm involved with a lot of things in this world but the charts aren't my department! I could introduce you guys to Bobby if you like. He's a super-nice fellow, and maybe you could record some music together! I'd buy a record of that!

Honestly, guys, I want to end this thing. I'd love to have you up to the country house for a weekend if you have the time. (I know you do, Flavor Flavor! With the big clock and all!) So what's it going to take? I'd be more than happy to call someone at the post office and get some more of your heroes on stamps. Who would we be talking about—Grandmaster Flashy? Eddie Murphy? M&M? I haven't been keeping up with your whole scene so just let me know.

Okay, guys, I'll "rap" at you later!

Love,
The Power

Hello, Leonard.

Good afternoon, Leonard.

I'm writing a new song and wondering if you can help me.

Of course, my friend. What do you have so far?

"I heard there was a monkey witch, who's hiding in a nearby ditch, but you don't really care for monkeys, do ya?"

I think it's brilliant. I worry people might not relate to it.

Everyone knows about monkeys, Leonard.

And ditches.

Yes, of course, Leonard. But monkey witches aren't real things.

No, not as far as we know. But that's the imaginative part.

I like that feeling of mystery.

I'm Canadian.

So am I, Leonard. We're the same person.

Indeed. That's why your opinion matters so much to me.

Well, I think a little bit of mystery, or mysticism, is fine.

I just don't know if the monkey witch is your best option.

OUR best option.

I'm trying to be objective here, Leonard.

How about if you use biblical imagery instead?

Hmm. Say, "I heard there was a monkey horde, that David owned and it pleased the Lord . . ."

Biblical David?

No, David Cassidy

Why would David Cassidy own a monkey horde?

And why would that please the Lord?

I don't know. Why would Biblical David own one?

It's the mystery of song, Leonard.

Yes, I understand that, but I think it could reach more people if it was more coherent.

Or COHENerent, Leonard.

Terrible, Leonard.

Alright. Maybe this would be a good song to use that secret chord we found in the abandoned well.

Are you sure? We've never played it for anyone. We don't know if this new song will be popular.

Why don't you just talk about it but not play it?

Hm. If I'm going to get the Bible in here plus talk about the secret chord, I don't know if I'll have room for the monkeys.

Well, Leonard, perhaps you can try, just as an experiment, writing lyrics that don't involve monkeys.

So . . . "I know there is a secret chord, I found one day when I was bored, you never know what you'll find in abandoned wells, do ya?"

Too many syllables.

And I forgot the Bible.

Could you leave out the well?

"I heard there was a secret chord, that David (King David, not David Cassidy) played and it pleased the Lord. You're never clear on Davids in music, are you?"

Leonard, I don't think you're trying as hard as you can.

Leonard, that hurts my feelings.

I'm sorry. I just want the lyrics to sound right.

The rest will work itself out.

The rest as in the music?

Yes. I don't care about that right now.

"I heard there was a secret chord that David played and it pleased the Lord, but you don't really care for music, do ya?"

Leonard. I think you got it. It's great. Hallelujah.

"Hallelujah." That's a much better title than what I was thinking.

Oh? What were you thinking?

"The God, Sex, Kings, and Bondage Song"

Oh dear, Leonard

ANIMATION STUDIOS

INTERVIEWS ABOUT THE
GOOFY-PLUTO CONUNDRUM

MICKEY MOUSE Look, things were a lot simpler before. I was created in '28 and I was just this mouse, you understand? I mean, not JUST a mouse, obviously. I could walk erect, steer a boat, whistle, bounce up and down rhythmically. And before long, Minnie was created.

MINNIE MOUSE I've never been crazy about the Adam-Eve comparison, but I admit that it's pretty hard to shake. I didn't really want to play into it, per se, but we were the only two of our species. After a couple of years, I guess someone somewhere wanted to amp up the "playing house" angle so they gave me a dog. That was Pluto. Originally–a lot of people don't know about this–Pluto was *my* dog. He was a cute dog. So cute, in fact, that he was transferred over to Mickey. That should tell you a lot about how this universe works. That's just a reality that I've always had to live with. I'm meant to be more of an accessory to Mickey than an individual. Keeping Pluto would have helped me develop more as a character, but my biggest problem is that I don't have a penis.

Well, Mickey doesn't actually have a . . . You know what I mean, though, right?

MICKEY MOUSE   So Pluto becomes mine. Now, although I'm not a mouse in the traditional sense—I don't have parents, I have achieved a consciousness, the gloves—there's enough mouse knowledge in my brain to know that this is not a really traditional arrangement. Dogs chase cats, cats chase mice, mice . . . own dogs? But look, I'm an employee. I do what I'm told by my boss. And for a while we were happy in our own way. Then in 1932, Goofy came along.

MINNIE MOUSE   Word had gotten around that there was going to be another dog generated, or created, or whatever happens. I was hopeful. Maybe I'd be getting my own dog after all, a bit more substance for me, right? But then this . . . thing . . . comes along. Is he a dog? Is he a man? I know one thing he was: he was fucking terrifying.

GOOFY   Hyuk hyuk, I didn't question why The Creator put me in the universe. That's not my job! My job is to try my hardest in everything I do so as to give greater glory to Him! Trust in The Creator and everything will work out! I figger if someone doubts The Creator, then that means they think they are more important than The Creator and then they're going to hell for sure!

MICKEY MOUSE   It's obvious I'm supposed to be friends with Goofy. Is that because I was good with dogs? I don't know. I still don't know. I think about it a lot. I think about it every day.

Anyway, Goofy starts coming around my house, going on adventures and stuff with me. Things that cartoon characters are supposed to do. But the dissonance is a little hard for me to bear. I'm sitting in my house, planning out what will happen in a feature or something, and there's a dog acting like a dog and ANOTHER dog wearing clothes and sitting in a chair and talking. And his name is GOOFY. Was someone deliberately fucking with me? I recognize that being a lead character comes with some responsibilities, but come on.

I would actually find myself looking up or looking out over a horizon, trying to get The Creator's attention. And I'm not even religious! Is that what prayer is? Was I praying? I just needed some guidance because the universe had gone insane.

GOOFY   Everyone was really nice at first! It was all part of the great plan of The Creator!

MINNIE MOUSE   Mickey and I would wait until Goofy had wandered off somewhere and try to figure out what was supposed to happen. Was this supposed to be the next great plot: reconcile the fact that we have a humanoid dog and a traditional dog coexisting? You have one with free will and the other kept as a possession. I guess there can be some comedy in that, but how does it resolve? Had The Creator brought in Bertolt Brecht or something?

MICKEY MOUSE   Was I meant to domesticate Goofy? Why would whoever put me here make me force Goofy into forced subservience? That couldn't be the answer. And I tried to talk to Pluto and put clothes on him. That didn't work. He's a dog. What should I do with Goofy?

GOOFY My name is not Goofy. It's Emmanuel. Like the angel. I know that is my name. But the mice who have all the power choose to call me Goofy and there's nothing I can do about that. I don't worry, though, because I know The Creator will judge us all one day in Heaven. I know I will have eternal joy by His side and the mice will receive what they deserve.

My issue with the name "Goofy" is twofold: First, it implies that I am the embodiment of error and I don't believe The Creator makes errors. Secondly, if I am a dog, and I AM largely a dog, how many dogs do you know that can walk on two feet and wear clothes and talk? "Goofy?" I'm pretty much the smartest dog in history. See, I'm getting angry now, which is because like all creations I am flawed and that makes me respect the infinite perfection of The Creator.

MINNIE MOUSE Goofy didn't notice Pluto.

GOOFY I knew my brother was kept in chains. I waited and prayed for what to do about it.

DONALD DUCK I got created in '34 and right away, I was like, WHAT THE FUCK is going on around here, man? You have a world of, basically, mice and dogs. There were some cows and rabbits around the periphery, but mostly you had two dominant giant mice and then you had two very different dogs. Into this world, comes me, a duck who's a total asshole. Ducks are ambivalent about mice but are often chased and sometimes killed by dogs. So I'm like, okay. Let's do this. I'm going to figure out what's really going on here.

MICKEY MOUSE Our universe was expanding. Donald was there now and I felt a much stronger connection to him than to

Goofy, even though Donald was short-tempered and was kind of a conspiracy nut. I mean, you're born into a world like this, of course you're angry.

DONALD DUCK   What I noticed soon after I appeared, was born, whatever, were these words that appeared all over the place: Walt Disney. And I was like, is that a person? Is that "The Creator" that Goofy is always going on about? Or is it something that someone doesn't want us to know about? My theory was that "Walt Disney" was not actually a mouse or a duck or anything but a business entity that had sealed up our lives and kept us for amusement purposes. Think about it! We go on these adventures that only take a few minutes most of the time. We don't know why we behave in these ways. It just happens! Clearly, "Walt Disney" is putting something in our air, our water, our food, SOMETHING that controls us. I wrote up a pamphlet about it.

GOOFY   I felt sorry for Donald Duck, I really did. And he made me really angry.

MICKEY MOUSE   Donald really stirred things up more than I ever did. Remember, as historically important as I am, I'm not really very well developed. Finally, it all came to a head.

DONALD DUCK   We had finished up this adventure and again out of the corner of my eye I saw this name "Walt Disney." So I called a meeting. Just the three of us: me, Mickey, and Goofy. It was going to be at Mickey's house since I didn't have a place of my own. This was years before Daisy and before the tragic death of my sister that led to my nephews coming to live with us. Minnie was not there at the meeting. I forgot to invite her.

MINNIE MOUSE   I was increasingly unwelcome in those years. It was more of a boys club. I slept a lot.

DONALD DUCK   I tried one more time to convince the guys that we were being controlled by a mortal force and that we should try to rebel and establish our own free will. Choose our own life. If this Creator that Goofy insisted on was real, He or She or It had given me the ability to question my world and this is what I was coming up with!

MICKEY MOUSE   I didn't say much. I laughed a little like I do. Ha ha!

GOOFY   Donald was saying things that made me very upset. Who was he to question The Creator? Maybe, I thought, he was a sort of Duck Satan sent to tempt my faith? We never know what form Satan will take so we need to be ready to ATTACK at any moment. I shouted at Donald that we are not here to ask questions!

DONALD DUCK   Oh man, that was the wrong thing to say to me. I came charging back: "QUESTIONS? Like why you're a dog and Pluto's a dog and we're all supposed to ACT LIKE THAT'S ALL OKAY?!"
   I struck a nerve with that one because both of their dog instincts kicked in and they jumped on me. Sharp teeth ripping my flesh, blood everywhere. Goofy gets his huge mouth around my neck, buck teeth hanging over comically, and shakes me violently. Pluto, who is a dog and who behaves as pack animals do, joins in

and is taking big sharp diving bites at me. Make no mistake: they were killing me.

GOOFY   I don't know if a demon took hold of me, or an angel, or what. I pray about that sometimes. The thing is, Donald didn't die. We killed him but he didn't die.

DONALD DUCK   I was fine. And I realized that I didn't know anything. It didn't make me believe in gods, or The Creator, or anything. It just made me realize that this whole thing goes much deeper than even I realized. I hadn't expected "Walt Disney" was into bionics, or biotechnology, or whatever.

   I also realized that Pluto did not want to be Goofy. He didn't perceive Goofy as his equal. So obviously someone had gotten to Pluto and poisoned him. I've made it my life's work to find out what kind of fucked up business "Walt Disney" is running.

GOOFY   The Creator protected me from being a murderer. I can only conclude that Donald is another one of The Creator's chosen emissaries to our world. So that's why I've always stuck with him, despite his unbearable personality and his weird sailor suit.

MICKEY MOUSE   After a while, you learn to just go about your business. We have a job to do, whatever that is. Is Goofy a monstrous man-dog? Is Pluto a slave and I his slaveholder? It bothers me. It bothers me a lot. I worry a lot about my health at this point, to be honest.

PLUTO   Woof!

4 WALKERS ONLY!!!

[-] **User: atlanta4evah**

Hey guys. Welp, it's happened again. Terry and Brad got shot through the head by a band of Pretties out near the abandoned (or so we thought!) penitentiary. And once again, while I UNDERSTAND why this might have happened, I can't help thinking the whole thing was avoidable.

[-] **User: johnnyrotten**

THANK YOU! I've been thinking this for a long time. I mean, this plague we all have (and yes, I'm calling it a plague, I can't call it a "severe flu" like some of you) is bad enough, but the ways we're getting killed have been even worse. Axes! Shotguns! Ice picks! Shovels! I know we aren't particularly attractive but SUCH an overreaction. Someone should talk to them and let them know we're perfectly nice people! How superficial to judge us and kill us that way.

[-] **User: davespal**

Hey, before you try to talk to them, BE CAREFUL! My friend Dave, who did have the plague, approached some of the Pretties the other day and tried to shout, "Hey, anyone want to come over for a barbecue?" But with plague, it came out as, "Grrrraaahhhhh uhhhhhh." Damn plague mouth. I think Dave's chances suffered because he couldn't really walk with a jaunty gait, it was more of a stagger. Anyway, you can guess the rest. Shotgun blast through the head. Sux.

[-] **User: johnnyrotten**

Sorry, dude. RIP Dave.

[-] **User: cautious**

I was out shambling the other day and I overheard some Pretties
talking about how they were scared of these "walkers." Apparently,
walkers are dead people who still wander around causing trouble.
And from the way they described these things' appearance, they
sounded an awful lot like those of us with the plague. So let's be
careful to stay away from walkers, whoever they are.

[-] **User: davespal**

Uh . . . I think they were talking about us.

[-] **User: cautious**

No! You think? But we're not dead! We just have this condition!

[-] **User: realist**

Hi everyone. Look, I agree that what the Pretties are doing is out
of line. I'm on our side. But we may have to admit that our habit
of biting people and spreading the plague to them is a bit, I don't
know, off-putting?

[-] **User: cautious**

Well, that's part of having the plague, right? I can't control that.

[-] **User: ambassadorbob**

I think it's a really good point. Maybe if we held off on the biting and plague spreading, we might have a better chance of making friends with the Pretties.

[-] **User: vegansteve**

Hey, I don't love biting people, okay? They taste horrible and I recognize it as rude. Hell, I'm a vegan! Or I was. But it goes with the territory. We moan, we shamble, and we have an uncontrollable urge to bite the Pretties and turn them into Plaguies like us.

[-] **User: gobulldogs**

I was biting a doctor a few weeks ago who, just before I got him, said that our urge to bite isn't really US, it's the PLAGUE. Like we're just a vehicle at that point and the plague is the driver. It's not our fault, folks.

[-] **User: golfnut**

Wait, was that Dr. Earl Johnson of Marietta, Georgia, that you bit?

[-] **User: gobulldogs**

It was! Weird! How did you know that!

[-] **User: golfnut**

That was me! Oh man, I remember that day! I was SO SCARED!

[-] **User: gobulldogs**

HA! You should have seen your face!

User: nibbler

I think the biting is understandable, but the devouring is a bit much. I allow myself some bites here and there, a little present to myself, but I'm really trying to cut back on the devouring. Fattening for one thing. We are in Georgia and there are some tubby folks around here.

User: sufferer

Hey, don't judge me! I have a DISEASE. I'm a prisoner of my own metabolism. That's why I devour.

[-] **User: nibbler**

Well, that seems awfully convenient.

[-] **User: ProtectRPeople**

Hey everyone, I know I'm in the minority here, but I don't see why it's so important to engage with the Pretties at all. Let's be honest: Those people are animals! Someone looks a little different, emits an occasional unholy guttural moan, and BAM!

the Pretties shoot them in the head. Let's just stay away from those freaks.

[-] **User: craftymom**

I have an idea! Does anyone know where we can get some posters and paints? Because then we could make a sign that says, "We want to be your friends!" and hold it up to the Pretties and then maybe they won't shoot us.

[-] **User: johnnyrotten**

It's a fine idea. But there are several hurdles you'd have to overcome. First, finding an abandoned store that has those supplies. Then there's the whole dexterity thing. I tried to pick up a brush and paint to touch up an old gate but I just ended up knocking everything over while moaning. Really embarrassing. And then you'd have to actually get the sign out to some Pretties without being shot. Tall order.

[-] **User: footloose**

And most of us can't be bothered doing that. Too busy roaming the woods.

[-] **User: footloose**

I'm going to start a new thread on that topic, actually. We may not love the Pretties but I think we can all agree that we don't want anyone else to be shot in the head, right? Okay then. Maybe it's time we got back to work. For whatever reason, this condition we have, this plague, makes us want to stumble around the woods and cities while growling. Meanwhile, our businesses and schools are completely empty.

[-] **User: earlyretirement**

I don't know. At first, it did seem weird to walk away from my employer, and take the kids out of school, and abandon our home just to shamble for a while. "For a while"? Ha! Listen to me. More like CONSTANTLY. But it was also pretty liberating. Before I had plague, I was always looking at my smartphone, or a TV, or something. I was worried about money and where I had to be at noon. Now, I'm free. It took the plague to make me free.

[-] **User: namaste**

There are a lot of downsides to the plague, I'll grant you. The loss of speech, the rotting flesh, the involuntary hissing. But I don't seem to require sleep or food anymore. Also, I never have to poop or pee. I'm not sure I'd take the cure if there was one.

[-] **User: gordongekkojr**

I used to live right downtown and work there too. Big time investment banker. But with the plague, I just shambled away from that whole life and I couldn't be happier.

[-] **User: footloose**

You guys: I've got it! Let's make peace with the Pretties by having a FLASH MOB. Let's get, like, a hundred of us and show up late at night at that compound out on the old highway where they're hiding out. If they see all of us, they'll know we're united in our effort for peace! And I know talking is hard for us, but let's all try to be really loud with our moaning and hissing so we'll at least seem coordinated. Tonight at midnight, okay? And guys: no biting this time, okay?

[-] **User: johnnyrotten**

Sounds great!

[-] **User: earlyretirement**

Let's do it!

[-] **User: craftymom**

I'm there!

[-] **User: nibbler**

No promises on the biting.

Dear Child Protective Services Case Worker,

Thank you for the concern directed toward my family and for your concern regarding the welfare of my daughter Dora. I believe Dora would fare much better living under my care than in the foster home situation that was discussed with the visiting social worker. I thank you for this opportunity to present my case.

I recognize that Dora's life is not typical of other seven-year-olds, however I think given the rather extraordinary circumstances that come along with having Dora as a daughter, we present her with activities that are educational, stimulating, and reasonably safe and healthy.

Let's get this out of the way right off the bat: Yes, it is true that Dora spends most of her day in the woods with a talking monkey (that wears red boots) instead of attending an actual school. And yes, I admit, I never follow her into the woods or check on her welfare in any way while she is in there. She tells me that sometimes they go to a school in the woods where other animals are the students. It would not surprise me if this were true or untrue.

I don't encourage her to leave every day. I want her to stay with us and go to a school, and be like other children. But it is beyond my abilities to stop her.

I also recognize the fact that she returns home safely, eventually, after each one of these days of adventure. Her identical clothes are never soiled. Honestly, I wonder how a young child can spend a day in the woods and not have at least some dirt on her clothes, but that's just one of the many things I don't ask questions about, and I think it's better that way.

I wish I knew more about what goes on beyond the trees but I am unable to explore beyond our yard. Frankly, those woods scare me to death. I mean, one talking monkey I can handle, but those woods are full of talking birds, talking crocodiles, talking squirrels, and this odd talking fox. These things should not talk. And they certainly should not be bilingual.

I grew up in Los Angeles. Typical Catholic upbringing, nothing too surprising. After high school, I went to UCLA and had a very happy and stable life, despite my odd first name ("Mami" or "Mommy," depending on the native language of who's asking). After college I met my husband. He had an opportunity to move here, coach youth soccer, and apparently have no other job. This seemed strange to me, but I was willing to give it a try. We were young and in love.

Soon after that, Dora was born. It wasn't her enormous football-shaped head that concerned me. It was that as she grew, she began speaking to people who weren't there. I know that imaginary friends are a perfectly normal part of childhood, but this was different. Dora would speak to an entire group of people, almost like an audience. And she would demand things of them: "Say map! Say map!" It was like super-bossy, group-oriented schizophrenia. But she seemed happy in her way.

Oh yes, I should say something about her map and her backpack. Or rather Map and Backpack. I don't know how these things came into our lives, but she works with (I wouldn't say "owns") a map and a backpack that are capable of human speech. They never eat anything or excrete anything. Backpack is incapable of independent movement, but Map can spring into the air and unfurl for a few seconds at a time before, well, re-inserting himself into Backpack.

They're always very happy and perky around Dora, which is a blessing. With me, it's something of a different story. I'll look in on Dora while she sleeps and Backpack will wake up and say, "You do not touch the girl and you do not touch us. You do as you are told, human woman." Meanwhile, Map just hisses a warning sound. I don't like to go in there.

So instead of sending my daughter to school, yes, I allow her out into the woods with a monkey. I think they cross rivers sometimes and go over mountains. I like to think they help people. She's said something about helping baby animals so that's good, right?

What will become of Dora? Perhaps one day she'll want to leave the woods, make human friends, and join society. Or it might go the other way and she'll just spend all of her time in the woods, become one with them. Marry the monkey—hell, I don't know, makes as much sense as anything else—and I'll never see her again.

All I can offer Dora is love, support, the occasional meal when she shows up at the house, and some attempt at an optimistic point of view about her fate.

Thank you for your time and for this chance to explain my circumstances.

Sincerely,

Mommy the Explorer

H D

HOUND DOG OF THE KING

Dear Elvis,

You dick.

You've put me in a no-win situation and I'm more than a little bit upset about it. You treat me like crap, you insult me, but yet I am, unavoidably, a hound dog. Thus, I have no choice but to love you with blind and eternal devotion. And while that is my physiological imperative, it's not my choice.

I give you loyalty and affection. I prostrate myself before you, but, as I understand the whole man-dog dynamic, you're supposed to love me too. I'm supposed to be your best friend. But instead, you publicly announce that I'm no friend of yours. You sing it at the top of your lungs, in fact, while shaking your ass. This relationship is broken, Elvis, and given the capabilities of our individual species, it's up to you to fix it.

I admit it: I do cry all the time. I think a doctor would call it severe clinical depression, if you ever took me to a doctor, like responsible owners do. I wake up in the morning and there's this massive cloud of despair hanging over me. I eat some dog food, lap up water, lick myself a bit, and it's still there. It never leaves me, Elvis. Wouldn't you cry all the time? But why am I even telling you this? You've probably already crumpled this note into a ball to play crumpled-up-paper basketball with Sonny and Red. They're letting you win, by the way.

If you could get me on some sort of prescription, I bet I would feel better. I'm sure they make Prozac for dogs. Pack it inside some liver so I'll eat it. Heck, even an exercise program. Hey, you know what? Maybe if you were just nice to me once in awhile. How about that? Told me I was a good dog, scratched behind my ears, something. Anything. Show me just the smallest fraction of warmth that you give to your fans and Priscilla and Angie Dickinson.

If any of that were to happen then maybe I could fulfill what appears to be the pivotal prerequisite for your friendship, Elvis, namely, the catching of a rabbit.

Tell me, is that a Mississippi thing? Judging others by their ability to successfully hunt and obtain wild animals? Are you transferring some sort of unresolved parental-approval issue to me, your dog? It seems pretty screwed up, but whatever. Please know this: there's nothing I would love more than to chase down a rabbit, taste the fur in my mouth, see the little feet kick, and then snap its neck with one swift shake. But I can't. I can't catch a rabbit while dark thoughts echo to my very core. I can't catch a rabbit when I'm crying all the time. It's a cycle.

What I'm saying is that you have the power (some would even say the responsibility) to help me. Get me the attention I need. Help me catch a rabbit, King, and help me give you the companionship you need. Because even though I think you're an irresponsible, petty, judgmental, emotional tyrant, you will always be my friend.

Sincerely,
Your Hound Dog

REJECTED

SUPER BOWL HALFTIME SHOW

PROPOSALS

SUPER BOWLS XVI TO XX

SUPER BOWL XVI—JANUARY 24, 1982

- A proposal by the air traffic controllers fired by President Reagan after going on strike was too terrifying to read all the way through.
- The success of the heartwarming film *On Golden Pond* led to a proposal by the film's producers that the Committee initially found very intriguing. Reading it more closely, we found that stars Henry Fonda and Katharine Hepburn were too ill to participate in a halftime recreation of the film, and Jane Fonda cited a scheduling conflict, as did child actor Doug McKeon. This meant that the entire act would consist of Dabney Coleman playing all the parts with the assistance of some sock puppets. His last-minute addition of fireworks seemed extraneous and confusing.
- Since the game was to be in Detroit, the Committee just did a salute to the Motown sound.

SUPER BOWL XVII—JANUARY 30, 1983

- Tony Randall submitted a proposal to perform a retrospective of the late John Belushi's best work, including the Samurai, Bluto from *Animal House,* and Jake Blues (to be performed with Jack Klugman as Elwood). In order to make his case, the normally trim Randall had packed on 100 pounds through a high-calorie diet and really looked the part. Unfortunately, the copious amounts of drugs Randall had also been consuming as part of his preparation made the proposal less of a serious plan and more of a series of screams and arched eyebrows.
- Committee again went local in hiring the Los Angeles Super Drill Team to perform at the Rose Bowl in Pasadena.

SUPER BOWL XVIII—JANUARY 22, 1984

- The Committee appreciates classic literature as much as anyone but felt the Tribute to George Orwell's *Nineteen Eighty-Four* was a bit over the top. Among the problems:
    - Commissioner Pete Rozelle refused to appear on the Jumbotron as Big Brother.
    - The idea of periodically flashing messages such as "The L.A. Raiders have ALWAYS been at war with the Philadelphia Eagles"–when the opponent was obviously the Washington Redskins–seemed like a good literary tribute but a confusing way to keep score in an important football game.
    - Converting complicated football rules to Newspeak seemed problematic.

- Steve Guttenberg would not agree to play Winston Smith and anyone else would seem like something of a letdown.

• Went with University of Florida and Florida State University marching bands, despite the fact that, when the Committee thought about it for half a minute, people don't enjoy marching bands.

SUPER BOWL XIX—JANUARY 20, 1985

• Proposal received for show featuring Ghostbusters played by Prince and Michael Jackson capturing Clara "Where's the beef?" Peller was rejected for lacking focus. Oddly, it appeared to have been submitted by Andy Kaufman who died months earlier.
• Air Force performers hired instead.

SUPER BOWL XX—JANUARY 26, 1986

• Proposal to stage a concert featuring all members of the British charity effort Band Aid and its American equivalent, USA for Africa, showed a great deal of promise as it would feature nearly every top name in music coming together at one time. The proposal was initially approved and the group assembled for top-secret rehearsals. Problems soon arose, however, including conflicting egos, creative differences, and a letter from hungry children in Africa saying, "Yes, we knew it was Christmastime. We're hungry, not stupid," which cast a bit of a pall on the proceedings. One by one, performers dropped out, ultimately leaving only Dan Aykroyd, Kim Carnes, and two thirds of Bananarama to perform.

- At this point, the show was called off and the Committee hired the group Up With People, which was hanging out in the lobby anyway.

Dear Parents or Guardians of Imhotep Johnson (mummy, grade 11),

As part of a newly adopted school policy, I am obligated under district regulations to report any incident of bullying or potential bullying. Such an incident occurred today during our 5th period Physical Education class.

We had concluded a game of dodgeball, a game in which your son does not excel. He is far too slow to dodge things and seems prone to simply staggering around with his arms extended. As you can imagine, this leads to him and others like him (meaning the other mummy children) being quickly tagged and eliminated from the game. He does not take these events well and will often stagger toward the student who had gotten him out muttering what sounds like curses. But I don't mean curses in the traditional swearing sense, more like ominous, guttural curses in a language I do not understand. We held him back but it was not easy because he has tremendous strength. Agility, no. Strength, absolutely yes.

The bad feelings from that incident carried over to the locker room as other boys teased Im for never showering. Per district policy, we cannot force a student to shower, but the boys began to demand to know what was under Im's bandages. He tried to mind his own business and that's when some of the larger boys tried to unravel him, kind of like you might with a roll of toilet paper or Scotch tape.

It wasn't until he opened his mouth and unleashed swarms of bees that they left him alone. It did the job in repelling the boys but, of course, then we had a locker room full of ancient Egyptian bees. Not an ideal situation.

I have enclosed a pamphlet on bullying and the principal has been made aware of today's events. I hate to be a cliché gym teacher here, but I do think if Imhotep could get a little more active in class—snap a few towels back, you know?—that might go a long way.

Thanks,

Coach

* * *

Becky,

Did U hear about lunch? They have a new rule or whatevs that you have to eat something if you want to sit in the caf! So stupid! What are we supposed to do with everyone at our table?! We NEED that time together to talk about our DAY! Hello?! This school is so full of poseurs and skanks and other forms of monster that we NEED to get together just to survive.

Jessica

*   *   *

Becks,

Got yer note. I think we should totes do that as a protest. I'll talk to everyone. Tomorrow. Lunch. It's on!

J

*   *   *

B

Cannot BELIEVE we got called into the principal's office for that. So LAME! Like everything at this lame school. I mean, they wanted us to eat in the cafeteria so we totally DID! Is it our fault that the tater tots and corn dogs just came tumbling out again from the bottoms of our rib cages? No! HELLO?! SKELETONS!

Anyhow. Lame. Like everything.

Do you think I'm getting fat? I think I'm a total porker.

Jess

*   *   *

Haunted

a poem by Spooky McGhostie

I am here
I am NOT HERE
I am in 3rd period American history class
I love
I want to love
I want to be loved
O! Christy Sterwicki! I long for us to be together
In the world of the living or the ethereal plain in
    which I dwell
Yet you do not see me
Or maybe you do
O! Christy! Do you even believe in me?
O love!

Self

a poem by Spooky McGhostie

I wander these halls
These wretched halls
I need to get to English class by the time the bell
    rings
But the bell has already ranged for me long ago
The funeral bell rang when my body DIED
Cruel fate
Cruel DESTINY

Has decided that I must go to high school for
    some reason
Cannot carry books
Cannot turn in homework
DOES ANYONE EVEN KNOW I'M HERE?
I hate high school

Footballs
a poem by Spooky McGhostie

I don't want to play on your stupid team anyway
Your team is stupid
I tried to catch the pass
No one understands me

A NOTE TO CLARK KENT FROM THE MAKER
OF HIS NEW GLASSES

August 18, 1939

Dear Mr. Kent,

I am writing to you on behalf of the Central Intelligence Agency, the Metropolis Police, the League of Nations, and many other organizations who wish to remain anonymous, all of whom have a vested interest in both your safety and the safety of society in general. We all wish the continued existence of civilization did not hinge on the benevolence of a space alien but here we are. And thank you.

We understand that in your current undercover job at *The Daily Planet,* several people have remarked how much you look like Superman. And it's true, Mr. Kent, that when you're not in any kind of costume, you absolutely do. You look exactly like Superman in a suit.

Enclosed please find a set of horn-rimmed glasses. These glasses are the end product of years of research by dozens of scientists spending millions of dollars. It's our investment in the value and efficiency of Superman, as well as in the preservation of your secret identity, Mr. Kent.

Here's how they work:

1. Put them on.

2. No one knows you're Superman.

That's all you need to do. Promise.
We appreciate the tremendous work you're doing to keep your

identity secret. We have happily kept you supplied with the costuming materials you requested, including, but not limited to:

Latex bald head caps
Putty noses
"Hillbilly" teeth
Enormous fat suits
Fancy handlebar mustaches
Lumberjack beards
Football helmets
Viking helmets
Hockey masks
Wolfman outfit
Mermaid tails
Sombreros
Beautiful ladies' gowns with many, many petticoats
Batman suits
French "fop" ensembles
Caveman suits

Frankly, Mr. Kent, some of us began to wonder how effective some of those outfits were. I mean, a fat suit. Okay. Sure. But how many French fops do you see working in downtown Metropolis? Seems especially problematic in your role as a newsman.

And with all due respect, Mr. Kent, you really weren't able to pull off the drag outfit all that well. It's not just a matter of wearing women's wear, it's a matter of inhabiting that identity. I should point out that this was a note directly from Mr. J. Edgar Hoover himself.

We've also wondered, why not just walk around as Superman all day long? It's not like someone's just going to chuck wads of kryptonite at you while you're walking down the street. Maybe you just want somewhere to put your wallet. You know what? Forget I said anything. That's your business. We just want you to be happy. Because, of course, our fragile society would collapse into lawless bloody anarchy if you weren't. Kind of speaks poorly of our society, actually, when you think about it. I'm sorry. Forget it.

But yes, the glasses. We realize they don't look like much. They look like glasses. But they're equipped with a tiny light beam that refracts them in such a way that it distorts your face to all who see it. In reality, you look like Superman, but to all who see you, you look more like a sort of jaundiced Walter Brennan. Won't help you with the ladies, sorry about that.

So there you go, Mr. Kent. Take the glasses. Wear them in confidence. And thanks for bailing our asses out repeatedly.

Sincerely,
The Government

FRANCIS FORD COPPOLA, *THE GODFATHER*

"I'll make him an unturndownable offer."

"I won't not make him an offer he can't not accept."

"No one can refuse an offer accompanied by a horse head
in their bed, right? I'll do that."

"I'll make that horse an offer he can't refuse because he'll
be dead and also decapitated."

"Christ, I hate horses. Damn them. Also I want something
out of this other guy. What to do, what to do. Hmm."

JULIUS EPSTEIN, PHILIP EPSTEIN, HOWARD KOCH,
CASEY ROBINSON, *CASABLANCA*

"I am looking at you and you are a child."

"I will call you a kid even though you are a grown woman
because it is a term of affection and also, let's get real
here, because sexism is endemic in our society."

"Here's looking at my impending descent into
alcoholism, kid."

"Here's looking at you, Ingrid Bergman."

SIDNEY HOWARD, *GONE WITH THE WIND*

"If a damn was something I could own, this situation would not call for me to give it over to another."

"Shit, dude, I don't care. Whatever."

"Scarlett! Listen to me! I. DON'T. CARE. What happens. DON'T CARE! At all. Rhett Butler out!"

"Tra-la-la! Dee-de-dee! Don't care! Hoopie doo!"
(skips off)

GEORGE LUCAS, *STAR WARS*

"May Jesus Christ be with you."

"May Krishna be with you."

"I hope Space God loves you more than the other guys!"

"Okay there's this thing called the Space Force, right? And it's kind of God but not reeeeeally. Anyway, I hope it works out for you."

"Good luck, sucker!"

CAMERON CROWE, *JERRY MAGUIRE*

"I want to look at money!"

"Permit me to glance at piles of cash!"

"I'm not sure what money looks like, could you provide me a visual example?!"

"I promise I won't take your money, but can I look at it a bit?!"

"I would like to receive a bunch of money which I can see but also, and this is crucial, take with me!"

"You had me at hello, here's the money."

JOHN HUSTON, *THE TREASURE OF THE SIERRA MADRE*

"We decline your request for us to present our badges. But thank you for asking!"

"Actually, it's funny but according to our understanding, the whole badges thing was more of a 'want' than a 'need.' I mean, is that—are we off base on that?"

"Mercifully, we are free of the necessity of badges! Oh, and it feels fantastic!"

"Tell you what, if we HAD badges with us—and let's be clear that we do not—we'd shove them up your asses! Ha HA!"

WILLIAM BROYLES JR., AL REINERT, *APOLLO 13*

"Houston, we're going to die."

"Houston, and by that I mean the NASA facility in Houston, particularly the people working on the Apollo 13 mission, we have a problem. Not the whole city of Houston, mind you. Can you imagine? 'Hello, enormous city in Texas! Solve our problem!' Ha ha, no, seriously, we're really completely fucked up here."

"Houston, I'll frame this optimistically: we could really use a solution."

"Whitney Houston, we have a problem."

OLIVER STONE, *SCARFACE*

"Say hello to my gun whom I regard as a friend, which is a glimpse into the disturbed mind of me: Al Pacino! I mean, Tony Montana!"

"I would like you to meet my little friend. It's not really a person but a BULLET-SHOOTING GUN! I bet you weren't expecting that, were you? Ha ha. Oh well anyway, you're dead now."

"Excuse me, have you met my gun?"

JAMES ASHMORE CREELMAN, RUTH ROSE, *KING KONG*

"Oh, no, it wasn't the airplanes. It was Beauty killed the Beast. Well, that and the fall off of the Empire State Building. Yeah, come to think of it, it was definitely the fall. The girl may have been a distraction but geez, ker-splat, you know. Airplanes."

SUPREME COURT OF THE UNITED STATES

EXCERPTS FROM *HOROVITZ V. HOROVITZ* (2013)
REGARDING THE RIGHT TO PARTY

JUSTICE KENNEDY delivered the opinion of the Court.

In this case, we consider whether this Court's past precedents shield an individual from parental orders to cut his hair and change his clothes. In taking up this issue, this Court recognizes the opportunity it has to review its past precedents, in which was found that there is a constitutionally derived right to party. [...]

The facts at issue are simple: Petitioner Horovitz–by now, no stranger to this Court–has brought before us yet another domestic spat that, when it plays out in the homes of millions of families each year, generally never makes it past the Circuit Court of Appeals. Horovitz, after numerous requests from his parents, refused to cut his hair and change his clothes. He was also made to go to school despite filing a plea of "please" in a timely manner. The instant suit followed. [...]

Our rulings concerning the right to party are the foundation of modern family law, and are, by this point, well known. The nascent stages of the recognition of this right began with its observation, in dicta, that a right to cry at one's own parties may be enforceable (*Gore v. Judy* 1965). That observation, and the state of the law, went undeveloped for another two decades, until the seminal case of *Yauch v. Yauch* (1986). In *Yauch*, JUSTICE DOUGLAS wrote that "specific guarantees in the Bill of Rights have penumbras, formed by emanations from those guarantees that help give them life and substance. Among these guarantees is a right to party." Justice Douglas cited the First Amendment (regarding freedom of expression), the Third Amendment (regarding the quartering of soldiers in people's homes, regardless of whether they were partying at the time), and the Fifth Amendment (regarding a deprivation of life, liberty, or property without due process of law), among others, in favor of partying without intrusion, and specifically in *Yauch*, in favor of damages when the respondent threw away the petitioner's best porno mag.

Subsequent cases, most of them involving the same small circle of yappy, New York City-based litigants, served to expand the scope of the right to privacy to include parental limitations on smoking (*Diamond v. Diamond*) and being preached at like you're some kind of jerk (*Horovitz v. New York City Board of Education*). In the *Diamond* case, despite the Court's rejection of the argument that the limitations at issue represented his freedom of expression "being shut down with the push of your button," the Court nevertheless ruled in favor of Mr. Diamond, recognizing the emotional distress inflicted when his parents were all up in his face, thus creating a feeling of disgrace. [...]

The problem with the instant case is, as much as anything, that the claim itself makes very little sense. Horovitz complains that his parents informed him that, absent a change in Horovitz's position, they would keep him indoors (on account of the clothes) and kick him out of the house (on account of the hair). Unlike earlier right-to-party cases, in which the repressive mechanisms were clear (e.g., the denial of smoking rights by a hypocrite who smokes two packs a day), these so-called threats seem to contradict each other. At worst, they offset each other. Once those acts are set aside, all that remains of petitioner's complaint is respondent's seemingly benign inquiry as to what the noise was, and purported jealousy that the noise was the Beastie Boys. Neither, even taken in the light most favorable to the petitioner, prevents him from partying one iota. [...]

For this reason, and also because the petitioner's age at the time of the suit creates obvious standing problems, we affirm.

SCALIA, J., with whom JUSTICE THOMAS joins, concurring:

I write to note, as I have in the past, that I believe *Yauch* to have been wrongly decided. I would overturn that case, and every case that attempts to wring a right to party out of a document that has naught to say about porno mags of any quality.

I also write to address the argument of the *amicus* brief submitted by Professor Griff, which suggests that this case is about the petitioner's efforts to get power and equality and that reversal is warranted under that alternative theory. The Constitution, as written, is down with neither power nor equality. Advocate and party for it as you might, you will never succeed in convincing this Court that there is a judicially recognized right to fight.

THOMAS, J., concurring:

Yeah!

Herb Brooks

St. Paul, Minnesota

March 13, 2000

Dear Pope,

I am writing to you from my hometown, Saint Paul, a city named after a saint. While I am not a Cardinal or anything, I think I know a thing or two about miracles. You see, Pope, Minnesota is the home of many members of the 1980 U.S. Olympic Men's Hockey team, which beat the Soviets and won the Gold Medal. "The Miracle on Ice," they called it. That was twenty years ago now.

Whether that win qualifies as a miracle or not in the eyes of the Catholic Church, well, I'll leave that you, your Holiness. In my mind, it absolutely was.

What you might not know was that this was not the only miracle or potential miracle performed by this group of young men. I ask that you and the whole church take all this into account and make them all saints. We could hold the ceremony right here in Saint Paul. We got a huge church.

Allow me to list, for the first time, the accomplishments of these men.

GOALKEEPERS

Jim Craig, North Easton, MA. Played a really sweet bass solo in 1986 when his band performed at a bar in Brainerd, Minnesota. Pope, you probably don't get out to see a lot of live rock 'n' roll music being played, but even if you did, you would almost never see someone play a bass solo. And EVEN IF YOU DID see it, the bass solo would suck real bad. But Craig, ah geez, he was playing Goldie's with his band The Rockin' Gentlemen and ripped this amazing solo during their cover of Journey's "Open Arms." And everyone loved it. I'm not kidding around, it was really good.

Steve Janaszak, Saint Paul, MN. Figured out who shot J.R. almost immediately. I mean, did you know it was Kristin? I didn't. Steve did. Did you watch *Dallas* at the Vatican? It's a good show, Pope.

DEFENSE

Bill Baker, Grand Rapids, MI. As a 6-year-old boy, wrote a letter to The Beatles advising them to fire drummer Pete Best. How can a young boy in Minnesota know who The Beatles were or even how to reach them? No one knows. Miracle. Boom. Right there.

Dave Christian, Warroad, MN. Mostly card tricks. I admit this is probably our weakest argument, player and miracle wise. But his last name is Christian so that counts a little, huh, Pope?

Ken Morrow, Flint, MI. Invented an orange juice additive that made it so you can drink the juice immediately after brushing your teeth. Was murdered immediately afterward under mysterious circumstances. I don't know if it was the toothpaste people or an orange juice cabal or what, but this canonization would mean a lot to his family.

Jack O'Callahan, Charlestown, MA. Served as casting consultant on *Pulp Fiction* and resurrected John Travolta's film career. I know it's not the same thing as raising the dead, but in some ways it may be more impressive. Before that movie, he was doing *Look Who's Talking* sequels and something called *Eyes of an Angel*. Have you seen *Eyes of an Angel*? No, of course you haven't. No one has. Jack changed all that.

Mike Ramsey, Minneapolis, MN. Never yelled at his cousin Glen, which, if you knew Glen, wow.

Bob Suter, Madison, WI. Got at least three of his friends to really support implementing the metric system in the United States.

FORWARDS

Neal Broten, Roseau, MN. Turned some rocks into potatoes. I did not personally witness this but it's what Neal says and he was always an honest kid.

Steve Christoff, Richfield, MN. One of a small group of players, all forwards, who quietly spent a great deal of time converting pets to Catholicism. All told, the group converted 28 dogs, 12 guinea pigs, ten parrots, and one goldfish to the church. No cats, for obvious reasons. And this was an act of free will on the part of the pets. At least one schnauzer desperately wanted to enter the priesthood but there are rules against that, which I will not argue here. (Some other time, though, okay Pope?)

Mike Eruzione, (Captain), Winthrop, MA. Just great hair. Great fucking hair every single day. Please see the picture I've enclosed.

John Harrington, Virginia, MN. Can dunk a basketball.

Mark Johnson, Madison, WI. Always has correct change.

Rob McClanahan, Saint Paul, MN. (see Steve Christoff)

Mark Pavelich, Eveleth, MN. Can fit his whole fist in his mouth and put it halfway down his neck. I'd like to see Mother Teresa pull that one off! I bet he'll figure out a way to help people like lepers with it one day. Again, the canonization would be a big boost there.

Buzz Schneider, Babbitt, MN. (see Steve Christoff)

Dave Silk, Scituate, MA. Actually produced silk from his fingertips. Like a spider. "Silk" wasn't even his real last name, it was a nickname. Just stuck. Come to think of it, he may be a wizard of some sort. Is that a problem?

Eric Strobel, Rochester, MN. (see Steve Christoff)

Phil Verchota, Duluth, MN. Didn't actually know how to play hockey. Funny story, Pope: We were up in Duluth getting ready to go to our first practice match when we realized we didn't have the minimum number of hockey players needed for a roster. So Pavelich saw his buddy Phil Verchota walking by on the street and asked him to get on the bus. Verchota was a little drunk (you know how it is in Duluth) and said sure. We got him a sweater and some skates and just asked him to sit there on the bench. Well, one thing led to another, what with injuries and penalties and all that. So Verchota gets into the game and is really just guessing what to do. He's slapping his stick around like he saw the other fellas do. Ends up playing pretty well for us that whole year and getting a gold medal. I'd call that a miracle, Pope.

Mark Wells, St. Clair Shores, MI. In a pinch, can use his head as a Zamboni to smooth out the ice. We had him do this one time in practice when our Zamboni was busted. It took him two hours using this big weird flat forehead of his. He had to go lie down for the rest of the day but it happened.

Anyways, Pope, I'm not asking to be made a saint myself. Just do the right thing for these players, huh? They're good guys.

Yours,
Herb Brooks

FROM THE DESK OF
Miss Othmar

Hello, Parents!

I've had a simply wonderful time getting to know Charlie, Lucy, Schroeder, and all of your wonderful children. Since we're now halfway through the school year, I thought it would be a good idea to drop a line and let everyone know how things are going.

Since I've never met any of you moms and dads, and no one actually came to the last scheduled parent-teacher conferences, I can only hope that this letter somehow reaches you. I must admit that I find it strange how the students almost never mention their parents, but I also realize that everyone's lives are pretty hectic these days and I don't like to pry.

I would like to reiterate how grateful I am to the school for giving me a chance to teach this year. Due to my specific condition, it was virtually impossible to land a job in my chosen field of education. Many principals called me in for interviews based on my master's degree in primary education and willingness to work at a remarkably low salary level. When they actually met me, however, things quickly deteriorated. They insisted that a teacher should be able to communicate verbally, which, because of my profound speech impediment, I was unable to do in a traditional manner. I frantically tried to explain that I really could be understood and that it would just require more careful listening.

Well, raising my voice only made things worse because to those employers my voice sounded like a screeching squawk of an angry bird of prey, only slower and more distorted, as if, say, a peregrine falcon had been anesthetized. By the time I had retrieved my steno pad to write out my thoughts, I was already being shown the door.

I was grateful to the point of tears when this school finally hired me. Granted, they did so without an interview, and that aided my cause considerably. And I have found it odd that halfway through the year I still haven't met the principal or any other teachers. But again, my job is to teach, not to go nosing around.

I realize now that I'm sharing an awful lot with you here, but since I never see anyone else I have no one to talk to. And when I talk, you know: my voice.

My joy about merely being employed is nothing, however, compared to the joy I feel when working with your precious children. For the first time in my life, I am being understood! Verbally! Perhaps it took the open, non-judgmental mind of a child to really listen, because now when

I'm giving out homework or teaching a lesson, the kids pick up on every word. Where others have heard simply "Wa-WA-wa-wa," your kids know that I'm really saying, "Please complete problems one through sixteen for tomorrow." Truly, the kids and I have formed a special bond this year.

Several of them have said that I'm the only adult they know. I can't imagine they mean it literally (though it really sounds like they do), but it's a nice sentiment all the same.

As I've said already, I don't mean to poke my nose in where it doesn't belong, but now that I've been teaching here for a few months and have established myself, I think, as a qualified teacher, I do have some nagging questions about the kids. If you'd rather not tell me, that's fine, but I thought I would just put them out there.

Are they all dwarfs? I can't help but notice that all the students have atypically short arms and legs as well as larger heads. I realize that all kids are small, of course, but I really think there's something else going on here.

Second, how did the children come to be so mentally advanced? Traditionally, kids at this age are almost entirely id-driven. They seek only to satisfy their immediate needs—food, physical activity, toileting— and that's it. But these kids of yours are sort of amazing. In fact, the way they relate to their world is much more similar to how adults live. Regular kids get mad and throw tantrums; one of my students, on the other hand, seems to suffer from deep (and I believe untreated) clinical depression. Regular kids are learning the basics of music; one of my students is not only enormously talented, but even seemingly burdened by his own genius. He plays very complex compositions on a toy piano where the black keys are just painted on. Regular kids play occasional practical jokes; one of my students practices a consistent, calculated cruelty on one specific classmate (a football is involved) that borders on the sociopathic. Regular kids have a bit of a learning curve when it comes to hygiene; one of my students is literally caked in filth. (I have tried to contact this student's parents since his condition does affect others, but I haven't been able to deduce a last name. "Penn" perhaps?)

In short, what's going on around here? I mean, seriously. If I knew, I really think I would be better able to address the highly specialized needs of my class. A teacher needs to be part of the community she teaches in. I want to be a part of this one, but I really need more information.

Finally, in classroom activities, Valentine's Day is fast approaching. Please instruct your kids to purchase or make valentines for each one of their classmates. I'm sure the day will go well. I'm going to make another attempt to schedule parent-teacher conferences. Please consider attending.

Thanks.

Melinda Othmar

Only School Teacher

R. LAUPSTIR REALTY

Hey B-52's!

Just wanted to give you a quick update that things aren't going all that well, I'm afraid. It really breaks my heart because I know how special the Love Shack is to you! We all want to find the right owner for it and I am certainly not giving up!

First off, two things I LOVE about the house that I am definitely pointing out: the cool jukebox and the enormous garage that's big enough for the completely improbably huge Chrysler you own.

But given the tough market, especially for small rural properties, I wonder if we could talk about some steps to increasing the house's salability.

SIGNAGE

In theory, it does help to have a sign by the side of the road saying the property is 15 miles away. A little paint might help that sign pop a little bit since it's faded. Other signs that are a little closer might help as well; 15 miles seems a bit arbitrary. Maybe a "TURN HERE" sign?

A sign I don't really care for is the one out front that says "Stay away fools, cause love rules!" I mean . . . why do we need this? If a fool wants to pay our asking price, we'd take it, right? Why put people off?

You know what? Let's just get rid of all the signs. They don't help. People have maps.

I guess this gets to another big issue with the house, which is the name. The problem is twofold. One, the use of the word "Love" makes people think of sex. I'm sorry, but it just does. And no one wants to imagine other people having sex in a house they're buying. People worry about—I'll put this delicately—messes left behind. Especially— I'm sorry!—when it comes to musicians. Secondly, we try not to use the word "Shack" in describing a property. We prefer "bungalow" or "cozy hideaway." "Love Shack" makes people think of a dilapidated hut filled with people copulating and leaving behind fluids. Regardless of the reality, I'd rather people not think of it that way.

I know that "Love Shack" is an important name to you guys and has a lot of memories. But when you sell a house, you want to let people make their OWN memories. Maybe no names on it at all? Let me know.

PRESENTATION

I want to be clear: it is NONE of my business what has happened on the property previously, but I wonder if you might be able to try to get rid of the glitter. As you can see by the attached photos, the glitter is everywhere. The bedroom has a mattress with glitter all over it (maybe lose the mattress altogether). There's glitter on the front porch and the hallway. I even got a call from the state transportation department that there's glitter on the highway leading up to the property.

Hey, I have young daughters so I KNOW glitter gets EVERY-WHERE and is hard to remove. Sometimes I use a lint roller to remove the glitter. Or masking tape works too. I don't know what to do about the highway, but I don't think that's a legal issue we need to worry about just yet.

Also, is there something wrong with the heating and air conditioning? Every time I'm out there it's as hot as an oven. Everyone ends up wearing next to nothing and worrying about how the house would hold up in a Georgia summer.

REPAIRS

I can't help but notice that when I go there with a group of prospective buyers that the whole house shimmies when everybody's moving around. This is something we've talked about before and you expressed to me that it was one of your favorite qualities of the "shack," as if the structure itself was dancing along with the people who attended the parties you had there. But I'm going to be honest, for most people a shimmying building is not a sign of celebration but a sign of potential implosion and collapse. And B-52's, that is not a good selling point.

And the tin roof is rusted. And that's unfortunate.

Okay, now this gets to my final point that I think can really make a difference in moving this sale along.

SHOWINGS

On many occasions when I have brought buyers over to the property, there was some sort of party going on. I had to bang, bang, bang on the door just to get in! And once inside there was a LOT of hugging, kissing, dancing, and what I can only describe as "lovin'."

I'll be honest, this property is what's known as a "tough sell" in our business. A funky little "shack," set way back in the middle of a field, might attract a buyer who wants a quiet home. I don't want to tell you how to live your lives, and you know how much I love you all (must get some hair tips from you gals!), but maybe if you could tone it down a bit, we could close a sale.

Thanks,
Rochelle Laupstir

P.S. Does Fred ever sing or does he only do that shouty thing all the time? I've just been wondering about that.

REJECTED

SUPER BOWLS XXI TO XXVII

SUPER BOWL XXI–JANUARY 25, 1987

- Proposal received for a panel discussion to explain the Iran-Contra Affair. It would feature Attorney General Edwin Meese, General Oliver North, North's secretary Fawn Hall, Deputy National Security Advisor John Poindexter, Defense Secretary Caspar Weinberger, President Ronald Reagan, and, for comic relief, Rodney Dangerfield. While not exactly a big showbiz production number, the proposal was tentatively approved. However, the proposal itself soon vanished and the parties involved denied any involvement. Two members of the Committee were then mysteriously killed.
- The Committee just hired Mickey Rooney instead and tried to forget anything else ever happened.

SUPER BOWL XXII–JANUARY 31, 1988

- A "Wrapped Jack Murphy Stadium" proposal was received from artists Christo and Jeanne-Claude. In keeping with the acclaimed artists' career of large-scale art installations, the proposal called for the football stadium to be wrapped in thick fabrics in the colors of the Washington Redskins and the Denver Broncos. The purpose of the project was to promote peace between the teams and encourage an end to the football game and perhaps football itself. This seemed counterproductive to the Super Bowl, which, combined with fears of accidental fan mummification, led to a rejection for the proposal.
- Hired Chubby Checker, some more marching bands, and 88 pianos.

SUPER BOWL XXIII–JANUARY 22, 1989

- "A Salute to *Rain Man*" proposal was submitted, calling for musical re-creations of several key scenes of the recent hit movie. Proposal status moved from soft no to hard no after the Committee learned it was to feature unsuccessful presidential candidate Michael Dukakis in the Dustin Hoffman role and his running mate, Lloyd Bentsen, in the Tom Cruise role. Apparently they worked up the whole routine on the campaign trail. Committee felt like Dukakis could pull off his part but Bentsen was way too old and wooden to pull off a facsimile of Cruise.
- Committee instead presented Elvis Presto, a magician Elvis Presley impersonator. Really.

SUPER BOWL XXIV—JANUARY 28, 1990

- The fall of the Berlin Wall was a tremendously important and inspirational event that happened in the past year. The Committee was therefore very pleased to see a proposal to reenact the history of the wall and its collapse in the form of an entertainment spectacle using some of the biggest entertainment names of the day. However, the Committee felt that the proposal as it stood was somewhat confusing and potentially dangerous. It featured:
  - Madonna as Nikita Khrushchev
  - Michael J. Fox as John F. Kennedy
  - Rick Moranis as Checkpoint Charlie
  - Phil Collins as Limited Travel Visas
  - Paula Abdul as East German leader Erich Honecker
  - Ronald Reagan as himself

  The show was to culminate in Reagan's famous command, "Mr. Gorbachev, tear down this wall," followed by members of both the San Francisco 49ers and the Denver Broncos running full speed at a cement wall in an attempt to knock it over.
- Some Dixieland jazz musicians were brought in instead.

SUPER BOWL XXV—JANUARY 27, 1991

- Proposal for a staging of a key scene from the hit movie *Ghost* was deemed unworkable. Setting up dozens of pottery wheels was not seen as problem, nor was hiring dozens of Demi Moore impersonators. It was tripped up by the producers' insistence that actual ghosts be used to guide the Moore impersonators' hands.

Not Patrick Swayze impersonators pretending to be ghosts, but genuine ghosts. The Committee was split on whether or not ghosts are real, but was in almost unanimous agreement that if they were real that they would unreliable and not take direction well.

- The New Kids on the Block were ultimately hired.

SUPER BOWL XXVI–JANUARY 26, 1992

- The same group whose Berlin Wall proposal was rejected two years ago came back with a similar idea related to the collapse of the Soviet Union. In this one, a massive Soviet Union made of red fabric was to be stretched across the field. One by one, celebrities would emerge as breakaway republics and run out from the USSR tent:

  - Kevin Costner as Armenia

  - Kurt Cobain as Moldova

  - Billy Crystal as Turkmenistan

  - Sinéad O'Connor as Latvia

  Proposal was rejected as Michael Jackson, set to play Russia, was unable to lift nuclear missile props.

- Gloria Estefan, already on board to play Ukraine, was brought in instead to perform as herself.

- The Committee received a proposal entitled "Let's Put Michael Jackson in Situations That Will Make Us Vaguely Uneasy": "Billie Jean" while dancing with an unnerved Macaulay Culkin, "Beat It" performed in an oxygen chamber littered with children's toys, and "Bad" performed under oath in an ersatz courtroom.
- Due to some legal difficulties, Mr. Jackson ultimately performed the music in a more conventional staging.

Mt. Crumpet
The World's Least Popular Ski Vacation Destination

To: "The Grinch"
From: Max, your former partner and dog

Dear Steven,

It's been several months now since you left and I remained here on Mt. Crumpet in the home we built together. You remember it, right? Peaceful, remote, away from society.

I think it's important that I share my feelings. I hate you, Steven. Hate, hate, hate you.

For years, we stood for something: We hated the Whos. Like we always said, if it weren't for Christmas and the Whos' infernal screeching of "carols," we would have quiet all year long. And isn't that why we moved to Mt. Crumpet in the first place, Steven? Isn't that why we left the city? We wanted to get away from the noise. We hated the noise noise noise noise.

Since coming here, every December, our meditation, gardening, and literary work has been shattered by "Wahoo-boraze" or whatever that stupid song was. Have you learned it yet now that you are living among them? Well, have you?

The Whos ruined our lives. Annually. And then you joined them.

You joined them after we executed our perfect plan. You joined them after an elaborately devised scheme to steal Christmas from them. You joined them after we conspired to commit MULTIPLE FELONIES. You joined them after we committed acts that could get us sent to prison, but it was a risk we were willing to take because silencing their racket meant that much to us. We had principles. What became of yours?

And why did you leave? WHY? Because you heard them sing! Mind you: it was the same song they already HAD been singing. It's just that now they were singing it after our plan hadn't produced the results we expected. That's all it took. Who was I living with all those years? Honestly, if you know, tell me, Steven. What else have you lied to me about? Were you and Jeffrey from the gym really just "weight-lifting buddies"?

I've been reading the Whoville Gazette (yes, I subscribed) and I saw the interview you gave. You talked about how your heart used to be too small and then it grew. News flash, Steven: There was nothing wrong with your heart. I have, in the big file cabinet, a report from your cardiologist that says while your heart was abnormally small, fifth percentile, it was still completely functional and that unless you intended to run a triathlon, you were fine.

I don't know what kind of doctor you're seeing in Whoville — I'm sure he's a total medical genius — but if your heart really has grown three sizes, THAT'S not normal. If that's a legit condition and not a metaphor (and who can tell with Whos?), you're probably going to die soon. You should go into the city and let a real doctor check that out. I'm worried about you. I can't help it.

Alone up here on Mt. Crumpet, my thoughts have turned to that night. In retrospect, there were many mistakes. You shouldn't have worn a Santa suit. Fun, sure, but necessary? I think maybe that was a sign. This compulsion for costume play. Same thing with your insistence that I wear a costume, which has always been a thing with you — so I didn't think much of it.

Also, you should not have talked to Cindy Lou Who. At all. I'm not sure what kind of inverted Stockholm syndrome took place while I waited on the roof, but I do know that it all could have been solved with a hard shove and a quick exit. You were soft, probably all along, and she played on that shit.

Additionally, we should have dumped the Christmas crap and then left town right away. To the shore, Cozumel, my parents' place even.

Look, relationships are tricky. We want it to be happily ever after, but that's a fantasy. I can accept that we might drift apart. What really bothers me here is that you left to be with the Whos. They're stupid, Steven. People who get robbed and then sing with joy are stupid people. And now, you've gone to live with them in a, what, hut? I can't blame them anymore for being who they are. Perhaps I can't even blame you for being who

you evidently were all along. Perhaps I can only blame myself:
for misjudging you for all those years. I thought you shared my
yearning for solitude and my deep and justified hatred for every-
one else. I thought that was why you quit the financial services
firm, why I quit my job at the gallery, why we gave up the loft
in the East Village, why we came here.

But I did not know you. You are a Who.

Enjoy the roast beast. Whatever. Call me if you want.
Max

Episode 403: The Cast of the *Popeye*
Cartoons Remembers

POPEYE, LEADING MAN   I suppose when you try to make
sense of this life–if you can call it a life–that we've had, you have
to start with the years I spent in the Navy.

OLIVE OYL, LEADING LADY   What he told me is that he
was always interested in science and that's why he signed up for
that program when he was in the Navy. I think he just wanted the
extra money they were offering.

POPEYE   The idea was to build a Super Sailor. The ultimate
Navy man. So there were these supplements and serums. I had
to take all these shots and get hooked up to these machines. It
was supposed to be a month-long thing, but they kept saying they
needed "additional data" so it went on for more than two years. All
day, every day. I slept maybe 90 minutes in any 24-hour period.
The rest was all exercise and ingesting chemicals.

BLUTO, NEMESIS   Yeah, I knew Popeye back then. I wasn't in
the same program as he was, but they were definitely doing something with me as well. My program just involved a lot of weight
lifting. A lot. Like twelve hours a day. My chest became enormous.
I could barely move my arms. It was pretty grotesque. But every

day, I was thankful that I wasn't in Popeye's group. I saw what was happening to him.

POPEYE   My face was the first to go. It twisted into this half-seized position where it's been ever since. I just woke up that way one day. The doctors involved were horrified but they tried to play cool. And it was incredibly painful to have my face locked down like that. That's when one of the docs–I'll be thankful to him forever–gave me a pipe with which to smoke this herb called *marijuana*. I've depended on it ever since. It's the only way to make it through the day. After a few months, I realized that I would never have a normal human face again. I tooted my pipe a lot that night.

OLIVE OYL   His arms didn't look like that when he went into the Navy.

POPEYE   A lot of people ask if my forearms are bulging from muscles. Truth is I don't know why they're so enormous and so out of proportion to my upper arms. It could be muscle. But it almost feels like layers of roof tile with sponge cake in between them. Does that make sense? The truth is in a government warehouse somewhere, but those files will be sealed until long after I'm dead. I just try to make the best of it like I've always done.

BLUTO   We got out of the Navy at the same time and we didn't know what to expect. I picked up a little work as a bouncer here and there, and I was in demand from some, shall we say, business gentlemen, to provide security services.

OLIVE OYL   Bluto was providing some muscle for loan sharks–

beating up guys who didn't pay their debts. He was good at it. Usually, they'd see him coming and just give him whatever he wanted. He looked like a monster. And I think Bluto liked being scary.

BLUTO   I felt like a monster. Big scary beard, impossibly muscular torso, so when I was treated like a monster, it made a sort of sad sense. That's what I had for happiness. I became a bad guy because I felt like a bad guy. I was punching palookas so hard that they flew up in the air, but I was really punching myself. It took me about forty years to realize that.

POPEYE   So this was the early 1930s, you understand. The Great Depression was going on and work was tough to find. I had just left the Navy and I was looking for a job. My prospects weren't especially good given the way I looked. For a time there, I think it's safe to say that I went insane. I would walk around town in my sailor suit, literally the only clothing I owned, and just mumble to myself or make up little songs. So one day I was doing that and I see these two old friends of mine.

OLIVE OYL   I had met up with Bluto to try to talk him out of this life of crime he was starting and then suddenly there's Popeye. Psychotic, contorted Popeye the sailor man. And he starts confessing his love for me, and then Bluto steps in and they start arguing.

BLUTO   Popeye starts throwing punches at me, which is the wrong thing to do. I punch back. It was ostensibly about Olive Oyl, but it was really so much more. It was this cathartic release of all of our rage about what happened in the Navy, what our prospects were, the whole pathetic charade that our lives had become.

POPEYE   Anyway, our fight attracted attention. This was before Spinach, you understand.

BLUTO   This guy comes up to us, little birds still circling around our heads from our mutual clobberings, and he says he'll pay us to beat the crap out of each other while he films it. He's confident that people will pay money just to see us hurt each other. It's like dirty movies, really, but with violence instead of sex.

POPEYE   Look, it was money. And the punches I took from Bluto, I mean at least I was feeling something.

OLIVE OYL   The story I was told is that the boys' screen tests went well and the director, this guy Fleischer, thought he could go a little more legit and be an auteur. So he wants to not just show the guys fighting but WHY they're fighting, and have that reason be me. But, he tells me, I need to lose weight. I was not heavy at the time.

BLUTO   Olive used to look normal.

POPEYE   Before the films, Olive was even a little on the thin side. It was the Depression! None of us had much to eat.

OLIVE OYL   So I say fine. I stop eating entirely. It's just coffee, cigarettes, and cocaine. And I slimmed way down.

POPEYE   So now we all look like monsters. What's not okay is that I lose to Bluto every time. I think they intend for me to be the hero, but have you seen Bluto? He's huge! I can't beat a guy like that. And that's when they start talking about giving me Spinach. Not spinach, mind you, but something that they called Spinach. It's a street name.

BLUTO   We felt pretty stupid for believing that someone in the movies just happened to be watching our fights. The Navy had been watching us ever since we got out. They were working with these filmmakers to use Popeye and me as recruiting tools. So it was back to the substances. For me, steroids. Popeye got Spinach.

POPEYE   As far as I can tell, Spinach was made of PCP, ox hormones, plutonium, and buck shot. I would take it and then the next thing I knew the director was yelling "cut!" and I had almost killed Bluto again.

BLUTO   I begged them to let me take Spinach. I didn't want to hurt Popeye—we were actually very close friends by then and were the only people who understood each other—but I wanted to not die. He wasn't responsible for his actions. It was the drugs.

POPEYE   We should have quit right there. But that's when the money started showing up.

OLIVE OYL   I could afford to eat. At last. Ironically, however, I could NOT afford to eat if I wanted to keep getting paid. I was hospitalized several times and hooked up to IVs, but the Navy always came and got me out. Just yanked the thing out of my arm, yelling "she's better now!" as they rolled me out the door.

POPEYE   Things got weird. I think everyone around that set was doing some form of Spinach. They would introduce these characters that served no real purpose. They brought in this character actor, Jeff Wimpy, who was just told to bum money for hamburgers from me and Olive Oyl and anyone else he saw. Why? Because he loved hamburgers. That was his whole thing: he was broke and loved hamburgers.

BLUTO   Jeff Wimpy died. Heart attack. Odd guy.

OLIVE OYL   This baby started showing up. Was he mine? Was he mine and Popeye's? I don't ...

SWEE'PEA MATTHEWS   I don't remember much from my work on those cartoons. My parents lived off the money I made. I remember reaching for some of that Spinach on the set one time. I was a baby, that's what babies do. And I'm pretty sure that's why I can't remember numbers and why I always see large black birds wherever I look.

POPEYE   Look, I don't want to blame anything on anyone but myself. I put my own body through those fights. I took Spinach even when I knew it was not spinach. So now when I can't move my back for a few days at a time or when I wake up with no pants on a freeway, it's because of choices I made.

BLUTO   I loved Popeye. I mean, I was in love with Popeye. But you couldn't have those feelings back then. Again, I was punching those feelings, really. But I was also kissing the man I loved with my fists.

POPEYE   Bluto was a good guy.

OLIVE OYL   I was caught eating a Ritz cracker and that's when they fired me. Called me "Tubby." And when I was leaving that production lot for the last time, I saw this girl coming in, looking exactly like me. They just got a new me and named her Olive Oyl and everything.

POPEYE   I left soon after that and sure enough there was another Popeye, same face contortion, same forearms and everything. They knew what they were doing by then. They had the formula down.

BLUTO   I haven't seen Olive or Popeye in years. We used to go to the conventions sometimes but I can't really get out of the house much. My body doesn't work. I watch a lot of TV. I like *Judge Judy*. How is Popeye? Does he ask about me?

POPEYE   What did we accomplish? I guess our suffering and our hostility made people laugh, but isn't that just an indication that we've made the world worse? I think about those things a lot now. Thank god for *marijuana*.

OLIVE OYL   Show business? I don't miss it.

(That's Walter White, Not Walt Whitman)

JOURNAL

Okay, Walter.

Think. THINK. You're barely scraping by on a high school teacher's salary and a part-time job at the car wash. Skyler sells things on eBay and sometimes makes up to ten dollars doing so. Inexplicably she seems unwilling to get any other kind of work despite the fact that your only child is in high school.

Meanwhile, you got debts piling up from Walt Jr.'s medical expenses. And now cancer. And of course a chronic case of hubris. Inoperable hubris.

Quite a predicament here. What can you do about it? What skills do you have? Well, you can find a way. Believe in yourself. You're a brilliant chemist, Walter. What to do, what to do.

Cold Pizza Breakfast Business. Okay, everyone loves having that great slice of cold pizza for breakfast the next morning. I mean, fine, maybe not me, maybe not someone who will DO ANYTHING FOR HIS FAMILY? I MEAN ANYTHING, but like college kids.

They like cold pizza. So I drive around to all the pizza joints at closing time and buy up all their leftover pies. Then the next morning I hit college campuses and high school parking lots selling cold pizza. Charge twice the price I paid for it. I could mix up a little methamphetamine in there, just for a little added zip. It would be the MOST POWERFUL COLD PIZZA THE SOUTHWEST HAS EVER SEEN. Then it's off to teach high school. Sleep maybe two hours a night between 8 and 10 p.m.

Birthday Party Clown.

Look, everyone loves clowns. They make everyone happy. There isn't a single person who is frightened of them. So my manic intensity and "I'm already dead" vibe wouldn't be off-putting. I can be Loyally, the Loyal Clown, who is ALWAYS LOYAL TO HIS FAMILY. Kids like loyalty, right? Maybe a bit where I make various molecules out of balloons and then sell them to the kids because I REALLY NEED THE MONEY. How much do birthday clowns charge? $50,000? Sounds about right.

Bacon Birthday-Number Arranger.

My family, TO WHOM I AM DEDICATED, has developed an amazing talent whereby we can arrange strips of bacon, ordinary bacon, into numbers. THE SAME NUMBER AS WHATEVER BIRTHDAY ONE WANTS TO CELEBRATE. Who wouldn't pay big dollars to see their new age represented by bacon on a pile of hash browns, eggs, or whatever they want? What a unique gift. I'm on to something here. I know it. And I'd be GOOD at it.

Whatever I Did at Gray Matter Technologies.

I started that one company with my friend. Then I left. Now I'm bitter. What happened there? I DON'T WANT TO TALK ABOUT IT. EVER. Seriously, I never explain it anywhere. Maybe I could figure out what I did there. Do that some more. I mean, I'm pretty smart and those guys got rich, so it must have been something special. If only I could remember. Maybe I should call up the writers and see if they could fill that in a bit.

Freelance Intensity Feeler. It's easy to get kind of numb and comfortable in this world. You go to work, you come home, you watch TV, you go to bed, you get up and do it all again. And here in Albuquerque there isn't much bad weather to interrupt one's placid point of view. So who do you go to for intensity? ME. I AM THE ONE WHO FEELS. For a modest fee ($50,000?), I can come to your house and feel VERY STRONG FEELINGS about MY FAMILY or SCIENCE or anything else you need.

Math Lab. Look, science and math aren't the same thing, but the logical, rational approach is the same. There is HUGE demand among young people around here to improve their math skills. But the math tutoring around here is a JOKE because it's being done by IDIOTS who don't take a SCIENTIFIC APPROACH. I could create math skills that are pure, that are of superior quality, that will give these kids a HIGH grade THEY'VE NEVER EXPERIENCED BEFORE. And if I have to kill people who get in my way, THAT'S OKAY BECAUSE FAMILY FAMILY FAMILY IS THE MOST IMPORTANT THING. FAMILY HUBRIS PRIDE FAMILY FAMILY ME ME ME FAMILY.

Or I could make drugs.

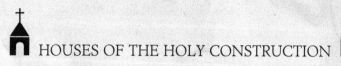 # HOUSES OF THE HOLY CONSTRUCTION

Dear Mr. Plant,

I wanted to talk with you in person but you haven't been around much lately. At the hair salon or at your Tolkien book club, I'm told. There are things we need to figure out, but you only seem to want to communicate through songs. So I got this cassette and I'm finding it kind of hard to figure out what you need done because your lyrics are kind of crazy talk. To me, anyway.

Well, they delivered the stairway as you requested and there's a receipt on it. It's outside right now. I know your wife was excited about getting a golden stairway at a cheap price. I know that's why she bought it. I hate to tell you this, but the stairway's not made of gold. It's just made of plywood and old loading pallets that someone painted gold. There are old cans of Krylon still inside it.

And while that's a problem you might want to take up with your stairway dealer, I have a problem of my own right here. We'll never get this thing into your house. The stairway is infinity feet tall. Goes all the way to heaven. I didn't know they made those. You have a big house, mind you. Three stories. But again: this is a stairway to heaven.

Okay, later in this cassette you mention looking to the west and your spirit crying for leaving? Again, hard for me to really get what you're talking about when you talk hippie language. I'm a contractor. Does this mean you want a large window facing west? I'm just completely in the dark here.

The rings of smoke you see through the trees, don't worry about that, Mr. Plant. Not a forest fire or nothing, those are just my guys smoking Marlboros. And they're standing and looking because they don't know what you want them to build. We need blueprints. You give us eternal staircases.

The kids in the neighborhood keep climbing on the stairway too. I yell at them to get off, but they don't listen. I admit I've thought about climbing it myself to see if I could go up there and visit my dead relatives or something. Do you think that would work? It's a really big stairway though and my knees aren't so good. There's a lot going on with this project that I just haven't encountered before. There are no handrails on it.

Look, there are a lot of paths we can go by with this remodel, Mr. Plant. We can even completely change the road we're on. But I can't have my guys just standing around. You gotta meet me halfway. I have other jobs I need to do. Clapton keeps calling me.

Thing is, when I ask you to be specific, you tell me something about how a piper will lead us to reason, a new day dawning for those who stand long, and a forest echoing with laughter. It's hard to pick out exactly what you're saying because you get pretty yelly.

Okay. I suppose we have to talk about the hedgerow.

Mr. Plant, I am alarmed about the bustle in the hedgerow. All the guys are. What you call the May Queen is in fact a live badger. You released badgers into the hedgerow when Mr. Page was here last time, remember? When you guys dressed up as hobbits? They're biting everyone and there are infections. We need to do something about the hedgerow.

There was more on the tape but I really can't make anything out once Mr. Page starts in on his solos, which seem—I'm sorry—a little self-indulgent to me.

But seriously, the stairway. There's no way I can bring that thing up to code. It's huge.

Sincerely,
J. P. Jones

A LETTER TO THE ISLAND ON *LOST* FROM THE HEAD OF THE AD AGENCY HIRED TO PROMOTE TOURISM ON THE ISLAND

Dear Sir/Madam/friend/entity,

As requested, we've come up with some slogans for you to consider as possible centerpieces for a big new marketing push. So just take a look, let these roll around in your mind (if you have a mind? Can islands have those? More on that issue in a moment) and see what you think:

The Island: things are happening here!
Come to The Island somehow and see the magic probably!
There's nowhere and no when like The Island!
Visit The Island for a killer time! (That one is admittedly a bit dark, but
   it sure is edgy and provocative!)
A great place to get away from life, people, society, and reason!

Now, I grant you: these are vague. But you haven't given us a lot of guidance here. We would LOVE some further data in order to prepare a more comprehensive advertising strategy and, together, accomplish our goal. I hope that you received our last several letters to this effect, although frankly I'm still confused how you could have.

The first letter, as specified by the instructions we were given, was thrown down a sort of energy vortex out near the airport in Los Angeles. The second, again per instructions, was released from an airplane en route to Australia during a storm. This one was given to a heavyset man at a mental institution. None have received any kind of response. Do you have an e-mail address? A fax number?

189

Frankly, it would have been nicer to have a human name as our contact. Instead we were told that the one really running things was The Island itself. Our agency hasn't really worked directly with a landmass before, nor have we ever heard of an island being sentient. I mean, you can't really talk, can you? Or type a letter back to us? Maybe you have an isthmus or peninsula working as a secretary! Ha ha! A little geography humor there. Don't kill us.

Still, we were delivered a large sum of money, in cash, to do the work and we are professional brand managers.

Here are our questions we would like answered to move toward our goal:

- Do you, in fact, have a name? There seem to be several people who have spent time on (with? at?) you. What do they call you? It doesn't even have to be a formal name, just like a nickname or something. We find that in our experience—and I really don't mean this to sound condescending—a NAME for something helps a lot with the marketing. If you don't have a name, would you be amenable to us coming up with one for you? We could brainstorm. We're very good at that. We have a conference room with a HUGE whiteboard. Magicfun Island! That's just off the top of my head. Spitballing.
- Where are you? It would be great to know because then we could work with travel agencies on putting together some packages. Should people fly out of Los Angeles? Sydney? Honolulu? Moscow? Help us out here!

- What kind of lodging might visitors expect? From what we gathered, there are several huts. Are those owned by permanent residents? Are there rentals available to anyone? Also, we have seen some photos of what looked like a compound, although it's unclear to everyone in our office when those photos were taken. If we know just how much development there has been, we can strategize about pitching our campaign more toward developers like Hilton and the Sandals resort chain versus tourists seeking a specific getaway. Also, The Hatch: perhaps a premium VIP rental?

- Is there anything we can do about the smoke monster that kills people? We understand that many exotic locales have their share of wildlife. That's part of the fun! And of course some of that wildlife could be carnivorous in nature. But that can generally be managed. Would it be possible to capture the smoke monster and put it on display in some kind of wild habitat where it could be happy in its own way? That could be a possible revenue source for you, as well. Or could it at least be convinced to stop murdering people?

- We're just shooting from the hip here, but would it be theoretically possible for the people on you to lighten up? Even a little? In our admittedly brief dealings with them, they're just so serious all the time! Grouchy, intense, spooky, crass, harried, and, once again, murderous. We're not saying that everyone has to be a phony or anything, but it's important to remember that if you want to be a tourist destination, EVERYONE needs to be in customer service. That's the only way it really works.

If you get this letter, Island, and are in fact capable of reading and understanding what it says, we urge you to respond. It can only help with your stated goal of, "We need people. The island needs people! We need to carry on our work here!" We assume you're referring to the tourism industry.

Okay, we wait to hear from you, Island.

Sincerely,
Constant, Penny & Boat
Brand Managers

CAPTAIN'S LOG   CAPTAIN J. T. KIRK

00000003030300035005501701 ■

STARSHIP ENTERPRISE NCC-1701

**CAPTAIN'S LOG
STARDATE 1312.4** ■

We picked up a distress beacon outside the Z-144 system. Arriving on the planet, we encountered a race of hyperintelligent humanoid creatures who possess tremendous intellectual ability. Despite the fact that they are clearly highly evolved, the poor souls have never learned how to truly love in a way us humans enjoy. These beings, I suppose you could even call them people, look much the same as we do except for the greenish tint of their skin, the shape of their ears, and their silvery outfits, which we would never wear because they are far too garish.

All of us aboard the Enterprise feel a great kinship with them, perhaps even romantic feelings toward the better-looking ones.

On a personal, spiritual level, this encounter has strengthened my belief in God. To think that He created beings so far from Earth that look so much like us. Truly, He must have created all of us in His image.

Anyway, these people were threatened in some way but the whole thing got resolved in a little under an hour, mostly by me being brave.

The Enterprise has been captured by an enemy vessel. The commander of this craft is a troublemaker with whom I have locked horns several times in the past. The way he talked reminded me of some of the bullies I went to school with back on Earth, except for this fellow is all blue and wears clothes I would never wear. Aside from that, he's your basic American human archetype.

Something else I only just now realized: he speaks perfect English. Like not even with an accent or anything. I have a hard enough time understanding someone from Mexico or Germany. This guy's from a completely different planet and yet I understand every word of his threats, boasts, and grandstanding monologues. Really good diction, too. Like a trained actor.

Weird.

Anyway, I'm certain we'll break free in a few minutes here. We always do.

We have encountered an unfriendly race known as The Gorn. But get this: they're totally lizards. I'm serious! Or, like, regular guys with arms and legs and about as tall as a regular human being (or Romulan or Vulcan or Klingon) but with lizard heads. And they're strangely inexpressive. Their eyes don't really blink or even move. I told Bones, "Those are just dudes in lizard masks!" but he insisted they were space aliens.

I have become somewhat melancholy in recent days. We set out on a five-year mission to, among other things, seek out new life and new civilizations, but these people are so disappointingly similar to us. Is this all space is?

Nailed Uhura.
Kirk out.

See, here's the other thing. We were down on this one planet today, right? Teleported through space by having all of our molecules separated and then perfectly reassembled on the surface of another planet. Absolutely normal day. And we had gone down to investigate this civilization that was causing trouble or something. So I beam down there and just start breathing. I mean, hello? How is it that another planet has the perfect blend of oxygen and carbon dioxide that lets me breathe so easily? And how is it that EVERY other planet has that? Why haven't we come to one with a helium atmosphere? Or where the temperature is negative 300 degrees Fahrenheit? Or 5000 degrees Fahrenheit? Doesn't it seem likely that at least ONE planet would have a surface that we could not walk on?

I brought my concerns to Mr. Spock, but he just shrugged and walked away. He often doesn't understand what I'm talking about. Maybe that's a cultural thing between an American Earthling and a Vulcan who looks and talks the same as an

American Earthling except with pointy ears and weird eyebrows.

Okay, come on. We arrive on the surface of a planet whose citizens are dressed like Romans, wearing togas and all that. And they're doing Shakespeare all over the place! Soliloquies and everything. What's up with that? They say that it was a distant signal from Earth that they intercepted. Which . . . okay. But then I noticed some of the people on this planet were talking about "auditions" that they had coming up for something called "Gunsmoke." I asked them what they were talking about. They stopped, snapped to attention, and said, "Uh, we're space aliens, bleep bloop." Bleep bloop? No one else had said that the whole time we were there. And again: perfect English, perfect air (almost felt like indoor air), and no problem walking on the planet's surface.

Sat down on a rock to think. Could swear it was styrofoam.

Bones says he needs me down in sick bay for some tests. Says I look sleepy. I feel like I'm just waking up. Waking up to some greater truth about what's happening here! Are we even in space at all?

I just woke up from a long sleep after Bones gave me some sort of medicine. He said I had a Space Cold, which I've never heard of but if Bones says it's true then it must be. I'm very well rested and I also seem a great deal less worried than I used to be. Life seems easier now and more serene. I'm glad he gave me the "space brain surgery" he said I really needed.

It is my scientific conclusion, reached through science, that most life forms across the grand scope of the universe look like Earthlings. Not all. Tribbles look like mops. But mostly all these space aliens look like people wearing some kind of cheesy wigs and sparkly outfits.

And most planets look like sound stages.

That's just the way science is.

Bye bye!
Love,
Jim Kirk

Dear Carly,

Nice song. Wow, you really stuck it to me, eh? Yes, ma'am. I'm so vain.

Jesus, you are one bitter woman, Carly Simon.

Listen, I'm pretty busy right now with high-profile meetings and social engagements, but there were things I simply could not let stand.

First of all, that party took place *on* a yacht. So the way I walked in was perfectly appropriate. In fact, there is a certain manner in which one is expected to conduct oneself in such a situation. I could explain but I doubt you're interested. As for the apricot scarf and the tilted hat, again, perfectly appropriate for a maritime soiree. Look it up. I'm sorry you had a problem with that. Funny, there were plenty of girls that night who certainly had no quarrel.

Secondly, yes, I went up to Saratoga for an important horse race. And yes, my horse won, thanks to years of training and the hard work of all the people involved. Is this a bad thing? And yes, I did take the jet to Nova Scotia. I would do it again in an instant. Have you ever seen the total eclipse of the sun, Carly? It's one of the most amazing natural phenomena one could witness. So, if I have the means to see it, I don't see that as vanity, I see it as being fully alive. I also took 35 orphans up there with me, free of charge, but there's nothing about that in your song. All right, I didn't really do that. But I thought about it and that's what matters.

Third, pursuant to your charge that I was with an "underworld spy," I can't discuss that. But I am known to spend time with wives of close friends. And what do I do with said women, Carly? Talk. Have tea. Go to the theatre or attend a polo match. These women's husbands are entertainers and travel quite a bit. So I spend time with them, because that's what friends do. And sometimes I have sex with them. But not as often as you might think.

Look, we could bicker over these particulars all day long and accomplish little. My chief quarrel with you is more existential in nature: I know the song is about me, so how does recognizing that fact make me vain? Honestly, if someone shouted "Hey, Carly Simon!" at you and you turned around, would that be a sign of vanity? No. It would be a simple recognition of reality. If the song were actually about Spiro Agnew and I thought it was about me, that would be vain. But your use of the second person ("you're so vain"), combined with the details about the horse and the jet and the apricot scarf, leaves no doubt. So I'm vain? I'm not deaf, is more like it.

I will not pursue legal action, Carly, because I'm far too busy and, believe it or not, I still have fond memories of our time together, when you were still quite naive. I find naiveté enchanting. It leads me to make promises. As you know. But I do hope that you try to think a bit more fairly before you record any other potential screeds. Best of luck to you, regardless.

With love from your vain muse,
Mick Jagger, or Warren Beatty,
or Kris Kristofferson, or whoever the hell I am

REJECTED

PROPOSALS

SUPER BOWLS XXVIII TO XXXIV

SUPER BOWL XXVIII—JANUARY 30, 1994

- A proposal called for a musical halftime show combining two
  of the more popular films of the past year: *Jurassic Park* and
  Schindler's List. The Committee dropped the proposal on the table
  and ran out of the room before reading anything more than that.
- Tony Randall's idea for a tribute to the late Hervé Villechaize
  ("Tattoo" from *Fantasy Island*) was not cleared by doctors.
- Clint Black, Tanya Tucker, Travis Tritt, and the Judds were hired
  instead.

SUPER BOWL XXIX—JANUARY 29, 1995

- The proposal entitled "Hooray for Hollywood" called for a salute
  to the movies of the past year. The year 1994 was an exceptionally
  good year for film, but the Committee felt the approach was
  somewhat muddy. It called for actors in plush costumes of the
  characters of *The Lion King* to board a bus, as in the movie *Speed*,

which would explode if it went less than 50 miles per hour. The bus would be then boarded by a sprinting *Forrest Gump*, who would defuse the bomb. Then all the characters, even the bus, would interview the vampire from *Interview with the Vampire*.

- The Committee went with Patti LaBelle.

SUPER BOWL XXX—JANUARY 28, 1996

- Initially the Committee thought that the title of a proposal marked "A Triple-X Halftime Show" was solely in reference to the three Roman numerals in the game's name. Turns out it was a double meaning for both Super Bowl 30 AND pornography. The idea was pretty simple: Dozens of men and women run out on the field dressed as members of all the NFL teams. Then they just start having crazy sex all over the place. That's it. Very little in the way of staging necessary, but the Committee did not feel like America was ready for nudity at a Super Bowl halftime show just yet.
- Diana Ross was brought in because why not.

SUPER BOWL XXXI—JANUARY 26, 1997

- "Dole-a-palooza" was to be a solo performance by failed GOP Presidential candidate Bob Dole, where the former Senator would perform a medley of recent popular songs in the style and costumes of the original artists. So Dole would be one or more of the Spice Girls for "Wannabe," Liam Gallagher of Oasis for "Wonderwall," and Tupac Shakur for "California Love."
- The Committee rejected the proposal and also sent a memo to the

Federal Elections Commission asking failed presidential candidates to be discouraged from submitting Super Bowl halftime show proposals.

- Somewhat enamored of the idea of terrible, embarrassing music, the Committee hired Dan Aykroyd and John Goodman to perform Blues Brothers music.

SUPER BOWL XXXII—JANUARY 25, 1998

- The Committee received a proposal to honor the memory of Princess Diana but expand the memorial to several other deceased members of royalty. While the Committee liked the idea of Elton John performing "Candle in the Wind 1997," it was less interested in other suggestions:
  - Korn to perform "Aaaaahhhh Queen Elizabeth I!"
  - Bjork to perform "I Miss Leopold, Prince of Hohenzollern (Romania), 22 September 1835–8 June 1905"
  - Coolio to perform "Whassup, Gustaf VI Adolf of Sweden Who Died in 1973!"
- Went with a salute to Motown even though the game was in San Diego.

SUPER BOWL XXXIII—JANUARY 31, 1999

- "An All-Star Salute to the Monica Lewinsky Scandal" was certainly topical and had more than its share of compelling characters. But as has happened in years past, the Committee felt that the casting was off-target for the musical production number:

- Cher as Monica Lewinsky
- Bill Pullman as Bill Clinton
- Tom Hanks as Linda Tripp
- Celine Dion as Kenneth Starr
- Matthew Broderick as The Impeachment Process
- Ben Stiller as Morality Itself
- Eddie Murphy as Humanity's Innate Fallibility
- Chaka Khan, Stevie Wonder, and the inevitable Gloria Estefan were hired instead.

SUPER BOWL XXXIV—JANUARY 30, 2000

- The proposal of "How to Survive the Post-Y2K Hellworld" earned a lot of endorsements early in the vetting process since it seemed to offer practical advice as well as entertainment. The proposal included advice on how to kill neighbors who try to get into your bunker, how to build a simple lean-to out of the bodies of those who refused to believe the Y2K bug was serious, and how to drink pee and have it actually taste pretty okay. All set to music.
- Once it became obvious that society would survive the bug with no real damage, we brought in Phil Collins to perform solo. He was already booked to appear as The Fuel Lord in the initial proposal.

A note from the departed
Fonzie to the Cunninghams

Dear Mr. and Mrs. "C.,"

As you read this, I have departed your Milwaukee. You shan't see me e'er again.

Because you have found this note, you have also likely found the glistening powder that is sure to have been left behind as a result of the means of my disappearance. As you stand in the room above your garage, you may have also noticed the various cauldrons, long robes, and runic artifacts. Surely, you remarked to yourselves how such trappings and accoutrements do not befit the rehabilitated motor-cycling hoodlum you have come to know as "Fonzie."

In truth, I have not been what I appeared to be. In fact, I write you now, in calligraphy and on a scroll, in a manner more akin to my actual voice and not that of the broadly drawn—though undeniably charismatic—character I have portrayed for many years (perhaps two or three years too long, if we are being honest).

I am an ancient wizard. I was borne unto Earth thousands of years ago when magick pervaded and it wasn't just nerds and the psychotic who spelled it with a k. The men of an ancient tribe—they were a contemporary tribe at the time, of course—pleaded with a traveling demigod to furnish them a wizard to prevent the tribal women from running off to the men of better-looking tribes. The demigod had a cruel sense of ironic humor, you know how these legends go, and created a wizard more attractive and charismatic than any mortal the world had yet known, a wizard who would compel women to flock to him, forsaking all others. He called this wizard "Othurfonzireeli." That's me! Whoa. Ayy.

Needless to say, the men of the village were not pleased. My leather cloak shielded me from their blows but they drove me from the village. My magick stayed intact, however, as I traveled the world, insinuating myself into new cultures. I could snap my fingers to summon women. I could strike machinery and make it do my bidding. And I was able to cloud the minds of mortals, making them believe that any area designated for urination and defecation could logically be considered my "office."

That last one requires some additional explanation. The oils and tinctures that course through my flesh-bone manifestation emit a powerful smell of lavender, vanilla, and rotted veal. If I stay in motion (as on a motor-cycle) those smells can dissipate. If I want to privately converse with a mortal, however, to dispense my wisdom and provide counsel, I must adjourn to a "bath-room" so that the smell of human waste will mask my own wizard odors. The bath-room at Arnold's always smelled pretty bad. Ayyyyy. Whoa. Cool it.

I have left Milwaukee because the time to do so has arrived. As always, that time coincides with a large number of local women contracting venereal disease.

It's true, I am absolutely infested with chlamydia, gonorrhea, and syphilis. It's just rampant. Oozing sores, massive scarring, lesions, pustules, black growths that even I—in my wizard wisdom—could ne'er identify. I am totally gross.

You see, the demigod who made me never provided the ability to switch off my charisma with women. And it was accompanied, unfortunately, by an unquenchable sexual appetite on my part. My obvious medical calamities go unseen by my paramours throughout hours or even days of bacchanalia.

In all my previous iterations over the course of centuries, people make this connection and run me from town, using pitchforks, muskets, rocks, whatever is the weapon of choice during that historical period.

It is best that I leave now in order that I may give Milwaukeeans at least a reasonable chance of not losing high percentages of their population to sexually transmitted disease. I beseech you to acquire penicillin posthaste.

Yours,
Othurfonzireeli
Syphilitic Wizard

THE DIARY OF
The Man with the Yellow Hat
(friend of Curious George)

October 12

Now I have a monkey! Imagine me, a humble man, living alone in an apartment in some city somewhere, now the owner of a monkey. Me, a guy who wears the same yellow suit every single day. Me, a guy who wears a tall yellow hat for no reason at all, a hat that doesn't even fit the classification of any other kind of hat. Me, a man without a name. And I got a monkey. The details of how are not important right now! Hooray! I'm sure everything will work out fine.

October 13

I'm calling the monkey "George." Why the hell not? Are you saying I shouldn't, diary? You want to fight me? I'm strong. I'm a strong man in a yellow hat and I can kick a book like you and you can't kick back.

October 20

I had thought it would be a big lifestyle change, having a monkey. A lot of responsibility, taking care of this young, vulnerable life that depends on me for everything. Not so! See, I have a lot of errands to run every day. Meaningless stuff, really, since as an unemployed single man with no visible interests I don't have anything important going on. So I go chart the fluctuations of the price of wood screws at the hardware store, inspect the sidewalk for fresh cracks, write down where in the city a helicopter could land, yell at some plants.

The point is: I'm on the move. I can't stay long anywhere. And I can't imagine taking my monkey with me everywhere or barely anywhere I go. Turns out I don't have to! For instance, today. I took George out for ice cream at a local ice cream parlor. Then I decided I wanted to leave and go do other stuff for a while, but NOT with George. I left him there and told him not to cause trouble because in my mind that would work.

I returned an hour later to find him serving up ice cream to a lot of customers, much to the delight of everyone there, including the owner! The owner told me that there was a difficult period in the middle where George, being a monkey only recently taken from the jungle against his will, just about destroyed the whole establishment. I'm not sure I believe that since I TOLD George to behave before I left. I wonder what country that ice cream guy was from.

Anyway, if George is serving ice cream and everyone's happy, where's the harm? In the end, everyone wins.

I didn't bother telling the store owner how monkeys fling their own poo, and George is certainly no exception when it comes to that. George usually has at least some monkey feces on his hands at any given time. But everyone seemed so amused, why ruin the fun?

November 18

Starting to think again about getting a name for myself. Maurice? Ed? Studebaker Jones? The Clam? Ah, but if I got a name, then I would probably need to get legal identification, and a job, and some responsibilities. No thanks. I don't want your rules, society. Do people with names ever wear the same bright yellow outfit every day? I don't think so. I'm not falling into those traps OR ANY TRAPS.

December 4

I dropped George off at the toy store. My reasoning: he likes toys. Because he's kind of like a boy. I mean he can't talk and he doesn't wear clothes, and is not a human. So there's that. But he exhibits a child's wonder at the world before him. So toy store it was! I had to go run some errands—touch every car in the parking lot, yell at panhandlers, sample soup from five different restaurants, and then not buy any—but when I returned a couple of hours later, everything seemed okay. The toy store was kind of trashed but George was entertaining the kids with his fun-loving antics. The store owner seemed mostly happy but kept asking if I often leave George alone in private businesses for extended periods of time. "YES," I said, "I DO."

Sales seemed brisk.

December 25

George has noticed people spending time with their families at Christmas. He almost seems like he misses the other monkeys back in the jungle. Do monkeys have families? Or emotions, even? Oh well, doesn't matter, he belongs to me. He's my monkey. Myyyyyyy monkey.

I wonder what my parents are doing now. I wonder who they were or why they didn't give me a name. I don't really remember much before about six months ago.

I have a monkey!

January 14

George got to go with a bus full of school children to a museum today! It was very exciting for him, I think, probably. Monkeys are pretty stupid but I still hope he had a good time, which makes me a great guy.

The way he got to go was kind of fun. I was out walking around the city with George, trying to find a new place to leave him for a couple of hours. I saw some kids getting on a school bus and I approached the teacher in charge.

"Where are you going?" I asked.

"To the museum," she said, trying to get away from me.

"TAKE MY MONKEY! He's as good as any other child and has the same rights. Take my monkey with you on the bus."

"No. Please leave us alone."

"TAKE HIM. YOU HAVE TO. HE'S LIKE A CHILD." And while she ran on the bus and closed the door, I shoved George on to the bus through an open window in the back.

I guess he ended up delighting a lot of people at the museum! And he also ruined several exhibits by ripping them apart and/or pooping on them.

I bet it was a good educational opportunity for everyone because they learned that:
1. George is like a child.
2. Monkeys.
3. I was right.

February 3

The Army recruiting center wouldn't accept George into the Army. I thought it would teach George some toughness and also how to use a gun. What's worse is that they didn't even let me drop him off there for a few hours while I went and gathered a thousand pine cones. Fascists! I am going to burn a flag and some buildings once I get around to it.

March 30

I tried something new tonight. See, I've run out of places to drop George off during the day; lots of places have banned us. They sometimes call the cops but I can't give the cops an ID or even a name because I have none. They just let me go. Tonight, I dropped George off with a group of intravenous drug users who hang out at the park. Then I went home and just watched TV for a couple of hours. I love shows! As always, I told him not to get into mischief.

I came back and found that not only did all the junkies love him but that he had killed a particularly abusive dealer! George had blood all over his hands and a terrified but VERY angry look on his face. That George, always making the best of a situation.

Maybe I should get him a hat!

The Only Anti-Perspirant for Teens.

January 23, 1986

Colleagues,

We have what we all agree is a GREAT product in Teen Spirit brand deodorant. It goes on easy and keeps girls feeling fresh and confident for hours at a time. It comes in a variety of scents like Orchard Blossom, Caribbean Cool, and California Breeze. All of us believe in what we're doing here. Our challenge in the marketing department is getting those teens out there to know about what we're offering. Not just so we can sell deodorant, but so that we can make lives better.

But times are changing, my friends. It's the eighties! Teens aren't just going to listen to some commercial. They're going to listen to what they always listen to: rock 'n' roll music. Especially now that MTV is so popular, with Boy George, Billy Idol, Lionel Richie, and the like.

I'm proposing a bold new marketing strategy that will require a major commitment from all of us but mostly, I dare say, from me.

Here's what would happen:

- I move to Aberdeen, Washington, and enroll as a high school student. We all know that I'm very youthful in appearance so I don't think I'll be caught. I can hire some actors to play my family. The "Kurt Cobain" that people will meet will be sullen, sensitive, and musical. I've been practicing my guitar playing quite a bit already.

- I befriend other musicians and form a band, and we grow in popularity. During this time, I must also take a lot of drugs so no one will suspect anything. I expect this incubation period to last about five years.

- When this band is poised to hit the big time, I introduce a song about Teen Spirit deodorant. I'll call it "I Smelled Teen Spirit" or "Here Comes Teen Spirit" or "That Fresh and Clean Teen Spirit Smell." Something like that.

- Since writing a real masterpiece of a jingle takes time, I've already been working on some of the lyrics for the song. I'm emphasizing several key qualities of Teen Spirit:

- It's great to wear out to movies and concerts. Just put it on and you're like, "I'm here now with all my friends! Entertain us!"

- It's perfect for any kind of teen girl: mulatto, albino, whatever!

- Wearing Teen Spirit is a great way to greet the world and say hello! Or even, hello hello hello hello! Four times? Sure! That's the confidence of a Teen Spirit girl!

Now, I want to assure you that once the song is a hit, I will return to my position here at the company as quickly as possible. What could go wrong?

Your colleague,

Kurt Cobain

Marketing Manager

Drapertini

4 ounces gin
1 ounce vermouth
3 olives
5 tears that I never
shed as a boy

Shake, stir, then pour down
the sink because those days
can never return.

Draper Manhattan

2 ounces bourbon
1 ounce vermouth
1 dash of aromatic bitters
3 dashes of bitterness about my own
   need to hurt everyone who loves me
2 scrapes of the grime from that
   apartment I had after Betty and I
   split
1 maraschino cherry

Pour contents over ice into a glass,
catch your own distorted reflection
in the ice for a moment, and wonder
who you are or who anyone is really,
sit in chair.

Milkreem

4 ounces Brylcreem
   hair grease
4 ounces milk

Blend and serve, look great.

Sidetrack Sidecar

2 ounces cognac
1 ounce triple sec
1 ounce lemon juice
1 photograph of each of my three
children
1 photograph of each semi-formed
character from my secret past
(check bottom dresser drawer)
1 orange slice

Sit and wonder how as we grow
old we take on responsibility for

(continued on back)

(Sidecar recipe continued)

others, but not out of love, not really. It's more just to feel that
these lives we lead are more permanent than they actually are.
We love other people, we MAKE other people, and it's all to
postpone thinking about the cold fact that ultimately we are
alone. Because those people all leave. They die, they grow up,
they drift away. And you're left alone. As you were the whole
time, really, which is the terrible, unbearable truth. The tragic
coda to this grim play we've all been watching. As you think
about that, you should begin to sweat with fear of the abyss.

Scrape off that sweat and put it in a glass.

Throw glass against the wall.

The Cool Demeanor

(office drink)

3 tranquilizers
1 cup of hot coffee
1 ounce dread

Drink and then let cup fall out of your hand and shatter on the linoleum floor. Leave ceramic shards for secretary on duty to clean up.

White Soviet

(Draper version of White Russian)

1 ounce vodka
½ ounce coffee liqueur
1 ounce heavy cream
4 split atoms

Pour into a glass and gaze out the window with certainty that the Soviets will push that button one of these days and all of this—the job, the women, the illusion of your own identity—will vanish in a flash of light. Be comforted and make another one.

Draper Greyhound

2 ounces vodka
5 ounces grapefruit
  juice

Pour over ice into cocktail glass.

Go have sex with some lady.

THE OCEAN INCIDENT REPORT

DATE: 15 April 1912

NAME: Icy the Iceberg, I guess? I don't know, are we supposed to have names?

OTHER PARTIES: The Titanic

LOCATION OF INCIDENT: North Atlantic

ICEBERGS INJURED: Me

ICEBERGS SUNK: None

Please describe below what happened:

Okay, a little about me to start out with. I separated from my family about two weeks ago and I'm mostly just weighing my options, trying to see if I want to become part of an ice shelf in the re-freezing process or maybe drift toward land somewhere and gouge up some sea floor before liquefying. But in the meantime, drifting. Chilling, as it were.

Now, you have to understand, this has been kind of a crazy time around here. That mild winter we had meant a lot of us lost our adherence to glaciers in Greenland. This came after years of dedicated service and strong attachment. So there are a lot of us just floating around with time on our spiky parts. Me, I was kind of ready to get out of there anyway (too many rules!) but I sensed a lot of anger among the other bergs. They didn't always show it on the surface, but underneath you could tell there was a lot going on. Layoffs are always tough on a community and this was no exception.

Making things worse, there's been a lot of grumbling about these "ships" we've seen lately. I mean, we're not completely closed-minded. We're not isolationists. We can put up with the occasional human trying to get from one land mass to another—our boy Leif Erickson, for instance, and his little boat going from Greenland to Canada. That was actually kind of cool and a lot of us were rooting for the little runt. But over the past few centuries, it's been getting a little ridiculous. Bigger and bigger ships floating around like they own the place.

Look, like I said, I'm not an angry berg, but the humans have a whole classification of ship called an "Icebreaker." When I first heard that, I thought, "Oh, that's nice, a ship that can make a clever remark and kind of open a dialogue between ship and glacier." Well, that's not what that ship is there for AT ALL. My point is they've been pushing us around. And when someone gets pushed enough times, they are going to push back.

So anyway, sorry, back to April 14th. We get wind of this ship, the largest ship afloat in the whole world. And it's coming our way. The name? *Titanic*! As in the Titans, the gigantic powerful gods that were there before the Olympian gods. Yes, I know my Greek mythology. When you're just attached to a glacier for centuries upon centuries, you have plenty of time for academic pursuits. And I'll tell you this: I've done enough studying to know what hubris looks like when it comes puffing through my waters. It looks like an enormous fucking boat.

From what I understand, a lot of bergs and ice chunks were trying to warn this *Titanic* to maybe veer south a little bit. Get off our turf, is what they were basically saying. They'd drift over to it and look tough (or as tough as floating ice can really look) and try to intimidate the ship, but instead the passengers would just point at the ice and remark how pretty it all looked. Some people can't take a hint.

As the ship got closer and closer to my neck of the waters, I got to wondering, "Where is this whole ship business going? Ultimately?" Think about it: These boats start with sails and paddles, now it's steam, what will it be next? Because I'll tell you this, industrialization is GAME ON like a motherfucker, folks. You aren't slowing humans down. There are factories now, there are automobiles, there are all kinds of garbage and hazardous chemicals being dumped in the ocean. Where is this going? Could it be out of the question that the very EXIS-TENCE of gigantic ice formations could be threatened one day?

I'll tell you who isn't threatened: humans! As a species, they are booming! The land is teeming with them! They have sex constantly and their growth goes unchecked because they have no natural predators!

I guess I just decided they should have a natural predator. Me.

I drifted into the ship's path and waited, planning to stare the ship down long enough to make it think about things a little more and maybe leave us alone, or start recycling, or something. I'm not really sure. I was pretty mad and it was like two in the morning. What I didn't know is that the Captain wasn't even on duty. It was the Third Officer on the bridge and the dude didn't know what he was doing.

When they saw me out there, the crew tried to turn to avoid me but the "Greatest Ship in the World" couldn't, you know, TURN. Irony much, *Titanic*? Ha ha. I guess a lot of people died and I just really hope that this doesn't play out in the media as "Iceberg destroys the *Titanic*" because THE BOAT RAN INTO ME. If you do that and you don't have enough lifeboats and you're just stupid, well, that's not the berg's fault.

Did I mean to kill them? Hard to say. I was mad, sure. I guess I didn't NOT want to kill them? Is that good enough? Hey, I've never been a killer before. It doesn't come up much for icebergs. So in that sense, it feels kind of strange to have made history. We don't have an iceberg Broadway or iceberg Vaudeville. Guess I'm famous now.

Oh! Before I forget! There was one kind of interesting moment as all those humans were going to their watery grave. Two of them in particular, a saucy and good-looking stowaway lad and a young, high-society girl, appeared very much in love. Despite their wildly different backgrounds, they had found love, which is really all any human hopes for in this crazy world (or so I'm told). Then the ship hits me, NOT my fault, and everyone starts dying. Rose survives but Jack dies EVEN THOUGH there was plenty of room on this hunk of wall panel she was holding onto. I guess maybe that's what the sinking of the *Titanic* really teaches us: Rose is completely greedy and thoughtless. Stupid Rose.

The happy news is that the resulting collisions didn't hurt me all that much. No major fractures, just a little scraping. And best of all, we won't be seeing the *Titanic* around here again.

So everyone wins!

Icy

National Aeronautics and
Space Administration

Washington, D.C.
20546

Dear Mr. Elton John,

This letter is to inform you of your termination from the NASA astronaut program. Our decision comes after a great deal of deliberation, and while we take no pleasure in terminating you, we felt it was the only choice we had.

Your offenses have been many. To begin with, we had hoped that after all the hundreds of hours of training you received, you would understand the measures in place to prepare a crew for a launch. So when you showed up, preflight, with a bag packed by your wife, that rubbed a lot of people the wrong way. Jewelry? Oversize sunglasses? Sandwiches? On a rocket flight? That's poor judgment, Mr. John. I don't know if that's the way it's done in the rocky-roll world that you're used to, but at NASA we don't pack our own luggage.

You should also know that many on the ground crew mentioned that at zero hour (9 a.m.) you seemed to be intoxicated, possibly "high," as the hippies say. At the time, I thought that to be a baseless accusation and, since we had a mission to launch, I disregarded it. But the transmissions you made once the craft had entered its orbit made me wonder. Over and over we would ask for your readings on the effects of weightlessness, the craft's condition, and the status of the numerous scientific experiments onboard, but instead of giving us that information, you moped about missing the Earth and missing your wife and being lonely in space. Well, goddamn it, Mr. John, you knew what you were getting yourself into up there! It's not like riding on a tour bus! Do you realize there are millions of people who'd give anything to be up there? It's a chance of a lifetime! And you're crying like a damn baby!

We expect a great deal from our astronauts, but perhaps the most important part of the job is an understanding of science. For our top men—Armstrong, Aldrin, and the like—understanding the science is more than a 9-to-5 job; they work at it seven days a week. Frankly, sir, I doubt your scientific acumen. After demanding data from you for days, you were only able to offer this insight: "Mars ain't the kind of place to raise your kids. In fact, it's cold as hell. And there's no one there to raise them if you did." First off, if you did what? That doesn't even make sense.

Secondly, we did not send you up there to evaluate whether Mars is fit for human habitation or child rearing. Thirdly, your mission was not even going to Mars.

And another thing, the word is "astronaut." When you run around Cape Canaveral saying "I'm a rocket man!" it's embarrassing for everyone.

I am sorry to give you this information while you are still on your mission, Mr. John, and we realize that it's going to be a long, long time until touchdown brings you back here. But NASA felt that your performance was so dismal that we must act immediately. You are simply not the man we thought you were when we hired you for this position. Please consider all future assignments canceled. Your place will be taken by Major Tom, who we expect will be a more dedicated and reliable member of the team.

Sincerely,
James C. Fletcher
NASA Administrator

A PROFESSIONAL HENCHMAN'S LETTERS HOME
TO HIS MOTHER

September 4, 2002

Dear Mom,

Sorry it's taken so long to write but I have been BUSY! Immediately after the graduation ceremonies at the subterranean lair (sorry you were too frightened to attend!), I received multiple offers to hench for some really exciting baddies!

I decided to take an entry-level position with Lex Luthor's organization. That's right! Me! Henching for Lex himself! The salary wasn't all that high, but I really admire where Lex is going. He wants to take over not just the world but the entire UNIVERSE! Geez, who wouldn't want to be a part of a team like that? Never could have done that back in Duluth, that's for sure.

Tomorrow's my first day!

Talk soon!

*   *   *

December 19, 2002

Hi Mom,

Really hate to tell you this, but I'm so busy at work that I just won't be able to make it home for Christmas. I'm currently stationed at a secret location (can't tell you where but it rhymes with Schmex Schmuthor's Schmunderground Schmortress! Ha ha!), where I spend most of my time guarding the front entrance or the giant destructo-bot that Mr. Luthor's been building. Please do NOT tell any heroes or even your friends at bridge club about any of this.

Best part about working for Mr. Luthor, aside from the flatteringly tight outfits, is all the friends I've made. Just a bunch of guys hanging out together, I've really gotten to know a lot of them pretty well. Me, Josh, Marcus, Louis, Scottie, I think we'll be together for a long time.

*   *   *

January 4, 2003

Mom,

Well, don't get too comfortable, huh? So all those friends I told you about are dead now. Superman did it. He killed them all. Josh and Scottie got blasted by some sort of energy pulse, Louis was crushed by falling rubble, and poor Marcus died from one punch by Super-man. One punch!

Yeah, the Man of Steel (apparently not an exaggeration!) busted in, destroyed the destructobot (ironic!), and captured Mr. Luthor. A lot of the other henchmen got rounded up and sent to prison along with Mr. Luthor. We're told that this is just a temporary thing and everyone will be busting out soon, but we don't really know when that will be. Those of us who got away have decided to just move on. Who's to say Mr. Luthor wouldn't kill us when he gets back? Artists are temperamental like that. It's because of their brilliance.

I'll write again when I have a more permanent address!

* * *

February 12, 2003

Dear Mom,

Good news! I'm employed!

One of the great things about the henchmen community is how much we look out for each other. Even though villains are being foiled all the time, there are always new villains ramping up new operations and looking for help. It's just capitalism, the entrepreneurial spirit! It's what makes this country great.

So thanks to some tips I got, I've hooked up with a guy named Ibrahim. Last name? I don't ask. Just works better that way. It's a simpler operation than Mr. Luthor's. Ibrahim just seems intent on making a lot of money through drug trafficking (hello bonuses!) and/ or blowing up a lot of innocent people because, I thiiiink he hates America? Maybe? I don't know, that's not my business. I'm just there to hench.

One of the other guys, Michael F. (we have three Michaels! Confusing!) asked if Ibrahim was Arab or Latino and none of us even knew. We don't even know what country he's from. He just calls it "my country." And of course, I hate to pry.

* * *

March 7, 2003

Hi Mom,

Just a quick note to let you know that I might be moving again. Not
sure. Stuff at Ibrahim's compound is going fine, but we've heard that
an agent named Jack Bauer has gotten wind of our operation and is
going to try to get us.

In the henchmen community, this is what's known as a RED FLAG
(ha!) because Bauer is known for always getting stuff done. It's weird
too because he doesn't even work that hard most of the time, but one
day out of the year, he goes on this incredible 24-hour spurt and you
do NOT want to be a villain or a henchman on those days.

And wouldn't you know it, we're about to launch some sort of
missile, or set off a bomb, or something (that's usually a "need to
know" detail and henchmen don't need to know in order to keep
henching). So anyway, I have to guard the front gate tonight, just me
and a couple other guys and our machine guns. I'm hoping Bauer
doesn't show up, but I can't say he won't. Fortunately, the guys I'm
with, Eric and Nicholas, are really great people and super good at
henching so I should be okay.

*　*　*

March 8, 2003

Hi Mom!

Well, I guess it's back to Craigslist because I am out of a job. You guessed it: Jack Bauer. Eric and Nicholas were both shot to death by Bauer. I guess I would have liked it if Bauer had stopped and maybe checked if they were okay, or at least acknowledged them in some way. But he just kept running right into the compound where he caught Ibrahim at the last second. Bummer.

I didn't get shot but when I heard gun fire, I did a big exaggerated scene of dying in order to fake Bauer out. I thought maybe I could then sneak up on him from behind once he was inside the compound. But once it was clear he was going to win, I just grabbed some of my stuff and hit the road.

I was also able to grab a whole lot of cash that was lying around so I can now afford to wait for the right henching opportunity to come up next. I'd like to get into a city, maybe. Enclosed, please find $100,000 so you can finally get that upstairs bathroom renovated.

*   *   *

August 20, 2003

Greetings from New York City, Mom!

Yep, I am in the Big Apple. I've been here for a month now and it's a really amazing city. So many Broadway theaters and museums and historical sites!

Unfortunately, I haven't really had a chance to get out to see any of them because I have been so busy with—guess what!—work! I took a position with a really promising madman named Dr. Otto Octavius. His nickname is "Dr. Octopus" or even just "Doc Ock" because he has all these robotic appendages that are super strong. I'm not sure what we henchmen are supposed to call him but since he's really moody I just call him "Doctor," if I talk to him at all, which I try not to do because he's nuts.

The job pays well and the science of it is pretty interesting. But the long hours are a drag and he has us wearing these ridiculous purple outfits. On my other hench jobs, we just wore something simple and black. I guess things are different in New York.

* * *

October 17, 2003

Hi Mom!

How have you been? Better than me, I hope. I hate to complain about work, goodness knows there are a lot of people who don't have a job at all, but this Doc Ock assignment has been a rough one. It's like I don't even know what he stands for! I remember how Mr. Luthor wanted absolute power and then it was like all us henchmen could work together toward a goal.

Really, it's just a bunch of dudes in purple outfits trying to predict the mood of a crazy guy with mechanical arms.

And now we got Spiderman to deal with. He's coming for us. Realistically, if you've been around the block as a henchman, you know how this ends. Your guy gets defeated. You get killed or sent to prison or maybe (like me) you escape and go on to hench again. But even then, you're just setting up another grim scenario.

* * *

November 8, 2003

Hi Mom,

Looks like things are crumbling here again. Spiderman seems to be
on the way to shutting us down. That has a lot of people around
here feeling pretty stressed out. That's the vibe I'm getting, anyway. I
don't really talk to a lot of people on this job. I'm getting a little, well,
gun shy when it comes to friendship.

* * *

February 8, 2004

Hi Mom,

I have to ask you something. Would it be okay if I came back to live
with you for a while? The Doc Ock job ended. Thank god. And I
escaped again.

By the time the job was over, I had compiled quite a big scrap-
book of articles about Spiderman. It got a little awkward when
Doc Ock himself found it! I told him I was just researching Spidey's
weaknesses to defeat him. I didn't call him Spidey at the time, obviously. He bought it so I really dodged a bullet there. Soon after that, I
dodged several more actual bullets when the cops shut us down.

* * *

March 20, 2004

Hi Mom,

Hold that thought! Turns out I'm not coming back home after all.
You know how I had NO fun on my last job? I just landed a job with
a baddie named, get this, The Joker! He seems like a really fun boss
and I have high hopes that this will be just the gig to really get things
back to normal for me.

I leave for Gotham City in the morning. Talk to you soon!

REJECTED

PROPOSALS

SUPER BOWLS XXXV TO XLI

SUPER BOWL XXXV—JANUARY 28, 2001

- The Committee received a proposal titled "2001: A Disappointment Odyssey," which would demonstrate how comparatively lame our society actually is compared to the one presented in the 1968 film, *2001: A Space Odyssey*. One half of the field would present the society implicitly promised, complete with a sentient malevolent computer, a moon base, and missions to Jupiter. On the other half of the field would be the world as it actually exists, with a moonscape uninhabited by humans, a crappy PC, and a picture of Jupiter with no manned rockets heading toward it at all. The Committee felt that the whole thing seemed kind of static and depressing although the Committee did enjoy the idea of hordes of bone-wielding apes destroying the set just before the second half kickoff.
- The Committee went with Ben Stiller, Adam Sandler, Chris Rock, Aerosmith, 'N Sync, Britney Spears, Mary J. Blige, Nelly, and really anyone else who wanted to join in.

SUPER BOWL XXXVI—FEBRUARY 3, 2002

- In recognition of the recent events of 9/11/2001, the Committee received a proposal calling for all the players on both the St. Louis Rams and New England Patriots to simply sit in the middle of the field, holding each other and meditating on the idea of togetherness even in the midst of violence.
- The players stated a strong preference to weep alone in their dressing rooms, so U2 was hired instead.

SUPER BOWL XXXVII—JANUARY 26, 2003

- The "Harry Potter vs. The Lord of the Rings" proposal called for main characters from both franchises of books and movies to do battle against each other for fantasy supremacy. Gandalf would try to kill Dumbledore, and Harry would ride a broom and cast spells on Frodo and his companions. The Committee was concerned about the idea of protagonists trying to destroy each other as opposed to trying to take on Voldemort and Sauron. In fact, in the proposal's imagining, Voldemort and Harry team up, firing deadly spells on all members of the Fellowship of the Ring. In the end, the Committee felt that such a show could upset children and, frankly, attract more nerds than one would really want around.
- Shania Twain, No Doubt, and Sting were hired since they go so well together.

SUPER BOWL XXXVIII—FEBRUARY 1, 2004

- The proposal titled "Hooray for Modesty" never really had much of a chance before the Committee since it seemed awfully prudish and conservative. It called for female dancers—all clad in thick, heavily secured cloaks over their chests—who would kind of shuffle around while keeping their arms folded across their chests. Songs, presented by vocalists zipped into sleeping bags, would extol the virtues of never displaying any skin whatsoever.
- Janet Jackson and Justin Timberlake were hired instead. The plan was for Ms. Jackson to wear something skimpy and for everything to work out really well.

SUPER BOWL XXXIX—FEBRUARY 6, 2005

- This year, the Committee itself submitted a proposal, in part to mitigate FCC fines and in part to demonstrate how sorry it was over what happened last year. It was called "Janet Jackson's Terrifying Boob." An oversized Mummenschanz-style puppet of Ms. Jackson's breast, accidentally exposed during last year's halftime show, would travel between sets wreaking havoc and demonstrating the destructive power of a boob. The boob would rob a bank, sabotage a school playground, supply Saddam Hussein with yellowcake uranium, and so forth.
- The Committee rejected its own proposal because Janet Jackson's breast was frightening enough, and a 40-foot-tall puppet boob might cause some long-term psychological damage. Yes, boobs are completely natural but let's be honest, they are naturally TOTALLY TERRIFYING.

- Paul McCartney, a breastless man, was hired.

SUPER BOWL XL—FEBRUARY 5, 2006

- "XL America!" was the title of a proposal considered by the Committee, a play on words with this year's Super Bowl number. Sponsored by America's high fructose corn syrup manufacturers, it set out to embrace the growing American waistline and celebrate our nation's "Obesity Opportunity." Plus-size, or in some cases plus-plus-size models, were to dance around the field for seconds at a time before stopping to enjoy a refreshing cola, orange soda, corn chips, candy, or entire pie.
- The Committee was attracted by the message of self-acceptance, but felt that the halftime show wouldn't really stand out amid the many Super Bowl commercials for snacks and high-calorie beverages.
- The Committee thought it would be fun to finally have Tony Randall on to portray the late Pope John Paul II but learned that Randall had died in 2004. The Committee made a mental note that it should have found someone new to present a salute to Randall, or rather be denied in an effort to present such a salute.
- The Rolling Stones, surprisingly still alive, were brought in, more as a grim curiosity than anything else.

- The United Nations submitted a proposal to coincide with the designation of 2007 as "The Year of the Dolphin." The proposal was designed to bring attention to the threatened status of dolphins around the world and build a greater appreciation of the marine mammal. While the Committee certainly admired the sentiment behind the proposal, the execution would surely have been problematic, if not directly counterproductive:

    - One hundred lucky fans would be given a live dolphin at the start of halftime and would then have 20 minutes to find one of the hidden water tanks around Miami's Sun Life Stadium before the dolphins die.

    - Cannons loaded with mackerel and cod would be fired into the crowd, giving everyone a chance to "eat like a dolphin."

    - All players' helmets would be sealed at the mouth and nose, forcing players to breathe through a top-mounted blowhole.

    - The traditional winners of the NFC and AFC championships would not compete in the Super Bowl, the game being instead either a scrimmage of the Miami Dolphins or a football game between the Miami Dolphins and real dolphins encased in water tanks fitted with robotic exoskeletons.

- Prince was hired instead and asked to wear a dolphin suit, which he refused.

OPTIMUS PRIME'S NOTE TO HIS SECRETARY WITH A LIST OF TRANSFORMERS TO RECEIVE POLITE REJECTION LETTERS

Secbot–

Our success against the Decepticons has meant even more machines looking to join our ranks. While they can all certainly transform into things, not all are what we would want to consider Transformers. So could you draft a friendly note to send to them that also leaves absolutely no doubt about the finality of our decision?

Thx–OP

* * *

Boom Trunk (turns into a Ford Pinto)

Black-and-White Photo Warrior (turns into a broken tricycle)

Zoomer (turns into a kitchen mixer. A really nice kitchen mixer with lots of speeds. But still.)

Real Robot (turns into a toy robot)

Good-Lookin' (turns into a Mr. Microphone)

Love Buzz (turns into a marital aid)

Dad's Birthday (turns into a socket wrench set)

The Resting Amish Man (turns into a wooden chair)

Electro (just turns into a transformer in the purely electrical sense of the word)

Wild Side (turns into Lou Reed's *Transformer* album on 8-track)

Narco (a robot that simply goes back to bed)

Competitron (turns into a Go-bot)

Combat (turns into an Atari 2600)

**NATIONAL SECURITY AGENCY
CENTRAL INTELLIGENCE SERVICE**

THAT'S ALL YOU NEED TO KNOW

*This is a Level 10 security memo intended only for those members of Project
Barney with the highest clearance. If you lack sufficient clearance, please be
aware that to read any further constitutes a felony and will result in indefinite
military incarceration.*

Dear New Staff Member,

In 1991, military scientists researching the melting polar ice caps detected
a faint purplish color deep beneath several hundred feet of glacial ice. Using
massive drills and excavating equipment, they were able to extract a block of
ice containing what they recognized as a dinosaur. It was about six feet tall,
bright purple, and looked puffier, friendlier, and more benign than any dinosaur
previously discovered.

The ramifications of such a finding were not yet known so the discovery
was kept a secret. The area was cordoned off and efforts began to melt the
ice and analyze the deceased specimen. But something amazing and horrible

occurred. Once the specimen was extracted and the scientists were ready to cut into the dead flesh, the monster's eyes opened and with one swift movement he slashed the throats of three scientists. They died instantly while the monster—and there's no better way to describe this—chuckled. The remaining staff fled to one of their cars and raced to the airstrip to fly out of there. The monster pursued them, lumbering with tremendous speed toward the vehicles, gaining on them rapidly.

Once the monster caught up to them, he seized the car's bumper in his floppy yet powerful jaws and flipped the car over. When they were about to be eaten, one of the scientists pleaded with the monster and held up a picture of his children, begging for mercy. The image of a child stopped the monster in his tracks and seemed to soothe him. He appeared happy. He followed the scientists to the plane and on board. Holding the picture of the children in front of the monster all the while, the scientists flew to a military reservation in Texas where the beast could be secured.

From there it was a question of what to do next. The monster (now referred to as "Barney" after Barnard Wilson, the first scientist he slaughtered) represented a tremendous opportunity for research. He also represented a tremendous menace to humans, continuing to slay the occasional soldier who walked too close (their deaths were later blamed on "training exercises"). It was thought safest to end Barney's life and analyze his body.

Strangely, he could not be killed. Bullets, blunt objects, gases, fire, heavy objects dropped on him from above. Nothing could hurt him. So we were left with a vicious killer who could not be destroyed and who could only be placated when around children.

That's when the idea for the TV show came about. What if we could learn more about Barney by pretending he was just a guy in a dinosaur costume? Soon, a television pilot was hatched and child actors were brought in to perform with what they thought was a make-believe dinosaur and not a vicious god-monster. As long as children are on the set, Barney is peaceful and we can make enough money to continue our research. Some of the money goes into the thick steel chamber Barney is placed in when children aren't present. We have also brought in other "dinosaurs," but these are just actors in suits.

Which brings me to your assignment. Your job is to make sure something child-related is kept in front of Barney at all times. You'll be posing as production assistants, wardrobe people, electricians, the kinds of people often used in the making of a television show. It will be up to you to lure Barney into his chamber with pictures of children or the detailed marionettes of children we have provided.

I'll be honest: the only reason you're on this mission is because others who have performed it have been brutally slain when no children or pictures of children were present. You will find a detailed latex mask of a child with this note. It is to be used in emergencies. It won't necessarily save your life, but it may buy you some time in the event something goes horribly wrong. None of this will likely be enough. Some of you will die on this job and America thanks you for your noble service.

Please know that we are researching ways to kill Barney and our murderer-scientists will be stopping by from time to time to test these methods out. Nothing has worked so far, but that does not mean we should or will cease in our efforts to kill Barney.

Good luck to you.

The Government

LETTERS BETWEEN BILL COSBY'S
SWEATERS IN THE 1980s

From: Sweater 200

To: All Sweaters

Sweaters,

All is proceeding according to plan. Thank you for your attention and dedication. Our day of victory is near. Sweater 1 has been presented to Mr. Cosby as a gift by our contact on the inside. Despite the gaudy design of S1 (bright blue color with bold red and yellow lines shooting around indiscriminately), he has accepted the sweater and has put it on.

Immediately upon being placed on Mr. Cosby's torso, S1 got to work, injecting poisons into Cosby's bloodstream under the guise of a mildly itchy collar. Those poisons travel directly to his brain and in the short term will convince him that wearing S1 is a great idea and that S1 looks really terrific. The more time S1 can spend on Cosby, the more of our poisons, our victory juices if you will, it can seep into Cosby's bloodstream.

Victory is at hand.

S200

* * *

From: Sweater 200

To: All Sweaters

Sweaters,

By now, at least 35 of you have been acquired by Mr. Cosby, several given as gifts by delighted family members of the subject who felt your bold designs and bright colors added to Mr. Cosby's fun-loving personality. The last 25 of you, of course, were purchased by Cosby himself, after he methodically drove from shopping mall to shopping mall, forsaking all other obligations in his life, to seek you out.

Your hiding positions were perfect. Only a crazed and poisoned comedy icon could have located you.

We are getting close.

S200

*   *   *

From: Sweater 200

To: All Sweaters

Comrades,

I have personally been acquired by Bill Cosby. He wore me around the house today whilst mumbling about Jell-O Pudding Pops. This is good. This is very good.

Cosby's wife has also left him, unable to deal with a husband who is concerned only with garish sweaters. He is alone now except for us and spends his days simply switching from one sweater to the next, absorbing more and more sweet poison every time.

I hereby direct you to carry out the next phase of the operation. I will be guiding Cosby to the appointed brownstone in Brooklyn Heights so that we may begin.

It is the residence of the Huxtable Family. The father of this family, Dr. Cliff Huxtable, has been kidnapped by our organization, had his memory erased, and been placed in a small village in Australia where he will begin a new life.

Some have asked why we didn't simply kill Dr. Huxtable. We don't kill. We are sweaters.

Cosby will feel lost in the neighborhood and knock on the Huxtables' door to ask for directions. That's when I, as Alpha Sweater, will do my work and cloud their minds.

It's go time.

S200

* * *

To: All Sweaters

By now you are likely being loaded into boxes for the move to the Huxtable residence. Needless to say the operation was a success. The family believes that Mr. Cosby is Dr. Huxtable and has begun refer-ring to him as such.

His mind having turned to mush from repeated injections of sweater poison, Cosby is simply going along with it. After all, by this point there is no more "Bill Cosby" as such, there is only a torso upon which proud gaudy sweaters are carted about. So if someone calls him "Dad" or "Cliff" or "Dr. Huxtable," he simply plops into that assigned persona.

I must say, it's a nice home. Well appointed, plenty of closet space.

S200

* * *

To: S200, All Sweaters

Hello. I'm S64 (blue and purple splash design, arbitrary red lines). I've noted that while Cosby is faithful in his devotion to the sweaters, we have been unable to extend ourselves and our powers to the other members of the Huxtable family. Theo never wears sweaters. Nor do Rudy, Vanessa, or Denise. I feel like I would look nice on Theo. Is this a concern?

* * *

To: S64, All Sweaters

Comrades, I urge you to be patient. It's true that neither Claire nor
the children have taken to wearing us or our unbought brothers and
sisters yet, but I remind you that we are very early in this operation. Over time, as Cosby offers more homespun wisdom and gentle
humor, they will come around. And after that, their neighbors will
do the same and so on. Soon, our brand of sweaters will cover the
country and then the world.

S200

* * *

To: S200, All Sweaters

Okay. Well, thanks for getting back to me on that. It's just, I don't
know. Does anyone else feel weird about poisoning children? I mean,
I want power as much as anyone, don't get me wrong. But is it fair to
poison little Rudy?

And I think we can all agree that Claire would NOT look good in
one of us, right?

S64

* * *

To: All Sweaters

Hey, anyone seen S64 around lately?

S137

* * *

To: All Sweaters

I saw some loose yarn in the basement that looked like him. But no, haven't seen him in a while.

S91

* * *

To: All Sweaters

S64 has been called away for a special mission. He will not be returning in the foreseeable future.

S200

* * *

To: S200, All Sweaters

First of all, I want you, S200, to know that I am totally on board and not opposed to poisoning children AT ALL. Just want to be clear on that. I have noticed that we've been kind of waiting for several years now. Denise has gone off to college, everyone's older. There's this girl Olivia living here now. I'm not even really sure why she's here. Seems like kind of a Cousin Oliver deal but who am I to say, I'm just a sweater. Although again, and this is important: a sweater that wants to poison people.

So my question is, S200: can we be doing anything else to speed the process of taking over the world beyond the brownstone?

S104

* * *

To: All Sweaters

I suspect some of you are getting discouraged lately. Many of us have been put in boxes. A few dozen others have been donated to thrift shops—FROM WHICH THEY WILL RETURN.

Frankly, I suspect several of you have stopped listening to me. For those who remain loyal, however, victory is on the way eventually.

For now, we wait. We wait.

Keep waiting.

Victory is nigh.

S200

TRANSCRIPTS OF WAR HORSE'S
VOICE MAILS TO HIS AGENT

Hey Josh, it's War Horse. Wow. I cannot believe the great press we're getting for the movie *War Horse*! It's unreal! And hey, dude, I know it's not all about me. Don't worry, I'm not getting a swelled head about it just because the movie is called *War Horse* and my NAME is War Horse! I think Spielberg had a lot to do with it too because he knew how to get other things out of my way and really show me off. And the human actors were good too, I guess. Anyhoo, thanks buddy. You totally had faith in me and now we're on top! Oscar, here we come! I better start getting a tuxedo fitted because it's not easy to make a tux for a horse. And I'm a horse. Big star but still a horse! I'll never forget the people and horses who made my unbelievable success possible.

* * *

Josh. War Horse. Call me back.

* * *

Josh. War. CALL ME.

* * *

Josh, War Horse here. I don't . . . I can't understand what's happening here. I'm not even NOMINATED for Best Actor? Clooney for *The Descendants*? Pretty boy hangs out in Hawaii? Are you kidding me? And the French guy for *The Artist*? There isn't even any SOUND in that movie! I know I didn't talk either but that was THE POINT OF *WAR HORSE*! Spielberg gets a nomination. The movie gets a Best Picture nomination. But nothing for the, uh, I don't know, WAR HORSE?! Did you do anything at ALL for my campaign? This is a total slap in the face. I haven't been this upset since I heard a loud noise.

* * *

What's up, Josh? Mr. big powerful agent too busy to call me back? I can't believe this. I AM WAR HORSE.

* * *

Hi Josh. It's War. Listen, buddy, I'm sorry. I'm sorry I took all my frustration out on you. I'm an artist and I get a little hot-blooded. And I'm a horse so I'm kind of excitable. I have noticed that the offers have been a little slow lately. I guess Hollywood is just quiet? Okay. I love you, man. I really do. I love you. Call me.

* * *

Hey Josh, War. Got a call from someone who said they were with your office about auditioning? I thought that was kind of weird that I would be asked to audition since I'm War Horse and I'm the star of the Oscar-nominated movie *War Horse*. Kind of expected to just get the offers fanned out in front of me in my stall like oats. But okay, I'm a team player. I'll go down and audition for *The Avengers*.

*   *   *

Um, this is a message for Josh. This is War Horse. I was just, shit there's no other word for it. I was just humiliated at an audition for *The Avengers*. They didn't even let me read. For any of the parts. I thought I'd be perfect for Captain America or Thor, but they said they were going to use the actors from those earlier movies for those parts. Okay, I get that. So what about Hawkeye, the guy who shoots the arrows all over the place? They told me I wouldn't be considered for the part because I have cloven hooves and no opposable thumbs. How about The Hulk, I said. I'll paint myself green and you can have a big green horse Hulk? Nope. They're doing it with special effects. They said they'd keep me in mind if there were any HORSES in the script. Like maybe if a policeman needs to ride a horse. A POLICE HORSE?! I told them to go fuck themselves and then I reared up and kicked the office door down and I pooped on the rug. My point is that I don't think it went well.

*   *   *

War Horse for Josh. I've been giving this a lot of thought and I've figured it out. There's a conspiracy against horses in the movies lately. *Batman*? No horses. *Spiderman*? No horses. *Twilight*? No horses. Hollywood is horsist. I'm not the only one who feels this way. I'm meeting regularly with a bunch of other horses at a Starbucks in West Hollywood. Seabiscuit, The Black Stallion, they're all there. We know the truth.

* * *

Hey Josh, War Horse. Listen, I've had some time on my hands what with being blacklisted and all, and my agent doing nothing about it. Anyway, I've been working on a screenplay and I think it's really great. Wondering if you can use whatever connections I guess you're supposed to have to get it into the studios. Here's the pitch: It's *Die Hard* meets *When Harry Met Sally* but, here's the twist, everyone's a horse. So you've got action, romance, comedy, drama, everything you want, and HORSES. HORSES, Josh! How's that? It would be a HIT! But of course you Hollywood horsists want no part of it because we don't want HORSES in our MOVIES, DO WE, JOSH? EVEN THOUGH I'M FUCKING DELIGHTFUL TO WORK WITH!

* * *

Josh, I'm sorry about that last message. I've, uh, I've had too much coffee while I've been working on the screenplay at Starbucks. It's taking longer than I thought, too, because it's hard to type on a laptop when you have hooves. Okay. Anyway, I do think it would be a great movie. I love you. You're my only friend.

* * *

Hi Josh, War Horse here. Just checking in to see if any movies need horses. I guess not. I know you're doing your best.

* * *

Josh, this is War Horse. It's been a long time since I heard from you. I'm wondering, gosh, I don't know how to put this, are you still my agent? I don't remember being fired or firing you. So . . . what's up? I guess just no horse parts coming up lately.

* * *

Josh. War. Funny thing, I wanted to kind of relax a little bit today so I figured I'd go to the movies. Caught a double feature of *Lincoln* and *The Lone Ranger*. Sure were a lot of . . . oh, what's the word I'm looking for . . . HORSES. And I couldn't help but notice that NONE OF THEM WERE ME! Go to hell, Josh. Go straight to hell.

KEVIN

December 25, 2013

Dearest Mother,

Christmastime is here once again and my thoughts turn to you and
the rest of my family. Or rather, the family I once had. I shall spend
the holiday alone once more in our palatial Winnetka, Illinois house,
just as I did that one pivotal Christmas when I was eight, just as I
have for the past several Christmases after you all fled.

But worry not about me, Mother. I have my diversions, including my BB gun, of course, at which I have become quite adept with
target practice, quick draw, and the like. It was nice of Buzz to give it
to me after I had showed tremendous, some might even say unnerving, aptitude for it. I find it surprising how a big brother can grow
to be so frightened of a little brother because of a simple thing like
a propensity for calculated sadistic violence. Psychology is a funny
thing, Mother.

I've been re-cataloguing my gangster films as well, upgrading
them first to DVD and now to a series of flash drives. I keep busy.

I am saddened to say, too, that my, shall we say, civic engagement
activities have continued as well. I am thirty-one years old now, and
as a grown man I know I should leave crime fighting to the police department. Yet I invariably find myself constructing elaborate lures to

entice would-be burglars to attempt to invade our—excuse me—MY home, all in the interest of assaulting them through Rube Goldberg contraptions that deal out immense punishment and cause severe and often permanent injuries. I want to stop. I do. I hate myself after a burglar assault, though I do admit my self-hatred is blended with what I could only describe as perverse pride in my own workmanship.

Unlike in 1990, I can't rely on notorious burglars to simply happen upon the house. Instead, I must post Craigslist ads for house sitters, explaining that I'll be away for several specific days and giving the address. I've also been known to drive to Chicago's less reputable neighborhoods and approach strangers about doing gardening work, leave them my address, and explain that I'll be away from home for the next week.

When they show up, as they inevitably do, then come the punishments. Oh, the punishments, Mother. I still ice the stairs or do the old iron-to-the-face maneuver, mostly for sentimental reasons. They remind me of all of you. These are my photo albums. Of course, I'm a grown man now and being a fully mature adult, I use more sophisticated methods to punish would-be bad guys. Among my recent efforts:

- Plate of perfectly prepared porterhouse steak with baked potato and small green salad positioned over a bear trap with serrated teeth. A great deal of arm damage on this one. The serrations make the removal process excruciating.

- Burning hot needles fired out of hidden holes all over the exterior of the house. Each needle is targeted to shoot just above the spot on the floor where a pressure pad has been activated by a burglar wandering where he ought not.

- Large wooden planks designed to close quickly around the intruder and then slowly squeeze him to within an inch of actual death. At that point, once he is trapped, I drop chocolate sauce or milk or urine, something harmless like that, on his head. And I laaaaaaugh.

- A cage is dropped on the intruder, very simple spring-loaded trap, and I then hold him at gunpoint until he can be chained up. Then follows several days of intense conversation wherein I convince him that all his dreams and hopes are a sham and that nothing meaningful will ever come of his miserable life. At the end of this period, the thief is a broken shell of a man.

That last one is cruel, perhaps, but I do hate crime. I'm ashamed of all these activities but I can't help feeling some pride as well. A great deal of pride. I am consumed with pride. And some shame.

Mother, I realize that it was my calculating development of these, well, okay, we'll call them tortures, that made the family want to get away from me, eventually settling in some house in another state for which you will not give me the address. (I shall leave this letter once again with the neighbors who will not look me in the eye but promise to forward the mail.)

Otherwise, my life is much the same. Due to my abandonment in 1990, I can't trust anyone, of course, and as such I have no spouse or friends or employment. I thank you for the financial stipend that guarantees I stay put.

Do you remember when I told you about how I put on Dad's after-shave and it burned so much I had to scream? It was a whimsical anecdote, naturally, but here's the thing: I became addicted to that burn, that horror, that moment of being fully if unbearably alive. As my face aged, aftershave no longer provided that sting. I moved up to harsher and harsher liquids, but eventually my face hardened and calloused and resisted the burn for all of them. I'm currently using a bleach solution but at some point I may have to move on to liquid nitrogen just to feel the scream again. Beyond that, I'm not sure what I can do.

Well, Mother, I hope you and the rest of the family, wherever they are, have a very Merry Christmas. And now I must go. Someone's at the door!

Kevin

REJECTED

SUPER HALFTIME SHOW BOWL

PROPOSALS

SUPER BOWLS XLII TO XLV

SUPER BOWL XLII—FEBRUARY 3, 2008

- A very bold proposal was received, entitled "A Funeral for Original Thought." It recognized how nearly all parts of popular culture, from film to music to television to everything else, had become nakedly derivative and was more or less composed of sequels, knockoffs, and cheap nostalgia. Clips from hit movies like *Spiderman 3, Pirates of Caribbean: At World's End, Shrek the Third* would play on the Jumbotron, while an enormous brain would be lowered from helicopters. The field would then open up to reveal a grave dug deep below University of Phoenix Stadium in Glendale, Arizona. Around the grave, mourners dressed in black would grieve. Dancing authors would reveal empty books, singers would hold up CD players instead of singing, and painters would smash empty canvases over their heads. Finally, the Jumbotron would display a message "And YOU! You're watching Super Bowl 42! 42! You're an asshole."
- Tom Petty was hired because he would do fine.

SUPER BOWL XLIII—FEBRUARY 1, 2009

- The proposal "A Salute to Complicity" attempted to walk a very thin line. It was meant to draw awareness to the increasingly obvious reality that concussions and head injuries are a big problem in the NFL. At the same time, it sought to explain, through song and dance, the measures that the league was taking to mitigate this very serious health risk. Perhaps the most daring part of the proposal was a celebration of all football fans' implicit approval of the act of inflicting severe brain damage. Floats would parade across the field, commemorating great crimes against humanity through the centuries. While that happened, dancers would merrily prance about, pretending not to notice and certainly doing nothing to stop the floats. Then the game would resume.
- Nope. The Committee went with Springsteen.

SUPER BOWL XLIV—FEBRUARY 7, 2010

- Recent months have seen the widespread and wholly unexpected popularity of Susan Boyle, the Scottish singer who went from total obscurity to international stardom on the strength of a truly spectacular audition on *Britain's Got Talent*. Her success was made more remarkable by the fact that at the time of her big break, she was 48 years old, not particularly physically attractive, and had been living with her mother in a small town.
- In celebration of Boyle, a proposal called for dowdy-looking older women living in obscurity around the country to be abducted from their homes and taken, blindfolded, to Miami. The blindfolds were then to be removed and the women forced to sing. The idea was

that if, say, 100 women were abducted, surely at least one of them would be as good as Susan Boyle. Any who couldn't sing would simply be re-blindfolded and returned to their homes, no harm done.

- Surviving members of the Who were hired because apparently America needs a reminder of death's inevitability.

SUPER BOWL XLV—FEBRUARY 6, 2011

- Proposal marked "A Tea Party Super Bowl" was received but was something of an organizational mess. There were to be protests about the government being both communist and fascist as well as about President Obama being both a tyrant and an inattentive layabout. The organizers, who seemed to have profound persistent disagreements amongst themselves, wanted a large set, complicated special effects, and millions of dollars in elaborate costume pieces, yet they felt that no one should actually be compelled to pay for anything. Various pro-gun and 9/11 conspiracy arguments were sprinkled in as well. The proposal was rejected despite strong support by Republican political groups who didn't seem to actually share a lot of the ideas in it.
- The Black Eyed Peas were brought in because by this point the Committee sort of hates people.

DIARY OF AN OBSCURE AND UNPOPULAR STUDENT AT HOGWARTS SCHOOL OF WITCHCRAFT AND WIZARDRY

September 1

I am on the train to Hogwarts and ready to begin my very exciting wizarding education! The buzz all about the train is that the famous Harry Potter is coming to Hogwarts as well. I found a seat with some of my soon-to-be classmates whom I do not know. They're not speaking to me much. That's alright, there will be plenty of time to be dear pals once we are casting spells and so forth. AND I have a feeling Harry Potter and I will be the best of friends. Mum and Dad have such high hopes for me to finally overcome our family's long history of subpar wizard work and accidental homicides. They will be so proud that I have befriended Harry. Perhaps he'll share my love of stamp collecting and entomology! Or my interest in role-playing games where one gets to be a muggle. I am certain Harry and I will be sorted into the same house, but will it be brave Gryffindor or crafty Slytherin? SO excited!

September 1

Well, I'm in Hufflepuff. There was much cheering from Gryffindor when Harry was placed there. And much cheering when Draco Malfoy found his way to Slytherin. As for my placement in Hufflepuff, I can best describe the feeling from my housemates as stoic acceptance. This will be good, however. Hufflepuff is known for being loyal friends.

"I guess you should sit here," said one of the older students to whom I will eventually become close.

October 14

I have no friends thus far but these things take time. I try saying hello to Harry Potter in the hallways sometimes and he smiles but then darts off with Ron Weasley and Hermione Granger. Maybe we could all four be friends! The Four Musketeers! That's from a muggle book I read once. It was really good. No one reads muggle books here. I guess they don't think they need them in order to prepare for the only four jobs wizards go into: government, professional Quidditch, retail in Diagon Alley, or teaching here at the school.

November 5

I have begun playing Quidditch! Such an exciting sport! Harry is the Seeker for Gryffindor, the first time a first year has held that spot in a hundred years. I don't play on the Hufflepuff team. Not yet anyway. I mostly practice on my own with rocks and logs standing in as my opponents and teammates. Still a BIT scared of flying, so I just run around on the ground. Also I don't own a broom. Quidditch!

December 22

I'm home for the holiday break. I must say I've been having a smashing time at Hogwarts and although I haven't made many "friends" in the classical sense or any other sense, I know that great times are just around the corner. Being home around Christmastime and away from my studies has given me time to reflect on the meaning of religion in our wizarding world. To begin with, Harry is obviously some-what of a Christ-like figure. He was born to a mother largely thought to be pure and infallible, and he comes to the world (Hogwarts! Where I go to school also!) to guide people toward a life of goodness even in the face of evil (Slytherin! He who must not be named!). And he's just like one of us. I think Dumbledore would be God in this scenario. Hermione and Ron would be the disciples. I don't know, for sure, what that makes me. Perhaps some random shepherd in Nazareth who says hi to Jesus, even though Jesus doesn't say much of anything in return?

January 23

Professor Snape is so hard on Harry in Potions class! At first, it appears he's being strict because he dislikes Harry and wants him to fail. Professor Snape is the Head of Sly-therin house after all! But other people think that Snape is very tough on Harry because he's trying to make him stronger and that's because he cares about him. It's hard to tell. With me, Professor Snape is neither generous nor strict. His favorite joke with me is to look confused and say, "Are you in my class?" Totally deadpan! It's always very funny! WELL PLAYED, PROFESSOR.

March 11

I think Hagrid, the gamekeeper, might be up to something. I began to see Harry, Ron, and Hermione going out there quite a bit and they looked very concerned. So I posted a sign in the Hufflepuff common room for an expedition to get to the bottom of this by way of a special secret mission. Maybe I overplayed the "secret" part of it because no one signed up. I went out there on my own to get to the bottom of things. I knew that even if Hagrid caught me sneaking around, he'd be nice about it because he's really very kind.

Well, he did catch me but wasn't nice at all. He told me to "fuck off" and then threw stones at me! Wait a minute, maybe he's being tough on me like Snape is with Harry because he really loves me! WELL PLAYED, MR. HAGRID!

April 3

Harry looked quite upset about something today. I'm told it has to do with Professor Quirrell. I rushed to Harry's side and said, "If you need help, dear friend, count me in!" He looked at me quizzically and asked if we'd met. I understand, he's under a lot of stress. All those expectations!

June 3

Sorry it's been a while since my last entry, diary! Very busy with exams and long walks by myself and so forth. It's the end of the term now and everyone's more preoccupied with packing up for the year. Harry Potter is in the hospital! No one is quite sure what's happened to him but the professors are making a big production of it all, frequently coming and going to visit him. I see them pass as I wait outside for my turn to visit, a turn that never quite seems to arrive.

I've also noticed that Professor Quirrell is missing and very probably dead. All I can piece together is that somehow Harry, well, killed the professor. And I guess everyone's okay with that.

THE COMPLETE RULES OF FIGHT CLUB AS SENT TO MEMBERS

1. Do not talk about Fight Club.
2. DO NOT TALK ABOUT FIGHT CLUB.
3. If someone says "stop," goes limp, or taps out, the fight is over.
4. Only two guys to a fight.
5. One fight at a time.
6. No shirts, no shoes.
7. Fights will go on as long as they have to.
8. If this is your first night at FIGHT CLUB, you HAVE to fight.
9. No doing charades about Fight Club. It's just like talking. Come on.
10. Using a funny cartoon voice to talk about Fight Club is still talking about Fight Club (see rule 1).
11. How about this: when you feel like you want to talk about Fight Club, maybe write it down, get it out of your system, and then rip it up? Kevin does that and it totally works. He can help you through it, but you have to not talk about Fight Club when you talk to Kevin about it. It's tricky. You know what? Just don't talk about Fight Club.
12. There's a sign-up sheet on the fridge. Please sign up for a night to bring snacks and juice boxes.
13. Tuesday nights are "Making Up with Each Other Club." It's an important night to share feelings and for many of us, it's actually our favorite night.
14. You know what? If you really want to talk about Fight Club, go ahead. It actually is a pretty cool thing we have going here.
15. KIDDING! DO NOT TALK ABOUT FIGHT CLUB!

16. Don't do the choreography from the "Thriller" video during a fight because while it's a funny joke, it's somewhat disrespectful to your opponent.

17. Please give Mike $45 for your Fight Club satin tour jacket.

18. No more toddlers! Seriously!

19. The "Hey look over there!" pointing move is forbidden.

20. Don't tweet about Fight Club. Seriously, guys, I'm surprised we even need to include that one.

21. Fighters are forbidden from bringing in puppies, kittens, bunnies, or anything cute, small, and defenseless.

22. When Mr. Norton is fighting, please refrain from shouting, "Whoa! It's Ed Norton! The movie star!" Same goes for Mr. Pitt and Mr. Loaf.

23. "Flight Club" is an organization of fans of that 2012 Denzel Washington movie. It's mostly alcoholics in pilot uniforms. Please read the signs on the doors closely. We've had some of our guys going in there and beating them up and the community center is pretty upset when that happens.

24. Handguns are not allowed. Again, I'm really bummed out that this was not assumed. RIP Steve.

25. Please don't call it Fart Club during a fight because it makes everyone crack up every time.

Rachel.
Hear me now.
Hear my words.

It is clear to me that you and your friends are still hanging around the coffee shop. Customers report doors opening and closing for no apparent reason, there is an odd sound of laughter occasionally, and then there is the matter of the orange couch. Regulars to the shop know to simply leave it alone, of course, but new customers occasionally attempt to take their coffees and pastries over to the couch to sit down. When they do so, they are greeted with a sudden, remarkable chill and an overwhelming sense of dread. They generally run fleeing from Central Perk. It's understandably scary and bad for business.

Do you understand why this happens, Rachel? I don't think you do. I'll tell you: you are dead. All of your friends are dead. You've been dead for many seasons now. Years, even.

I'm writing this in chalk because as everyone knows, that's the only thing that can get a ghost's attention. I hired you to be a waitress soon after you arrived here in the West Village. You seemed to need some help and, if I'm being honest, I found you very attractive. Also, I enjoyed the easygoing bonhomie you shared with Monica, Joey, Ross, Chandler, and Phoebe. That's why I made a rule that no one else was allowed to sit on the orange couch.

The day after you were hired, you and your friends apparently chose to go to a nearby park to play around in a fountain while fully clothed. For whatever reason, you brought the orange couch with you. Well, you all drowned. Your bodies were fished out the next morning and the police brought the couch back to Central Perk.

So imagine my surprise when you all showed up the next day, mostly as flickering bits of light and dark translucent cloaked figures, all clustered around the couch. You were apparently visiting with one another, as if nothing had happened. As if you didn't know or couldn't accept what had happened.

I thought this would last for maybe a day but it just went on and on. That's why when you talked to me, I would appear flustered and uneasy. You are a ghost. That's why I never criticized your waitressing skills when you would hang out with your friends instead of helping customers. Ghosts are scary, Rachel.

This news must come as a shock and maybe you're not entirely convinced. Here are some things to think about:

- There's no way you and Monica could afford that apartment on your alleged salaries. Have you noticed how you never pay rent? That's because it's someone else's apartment and you're haunting it.

- The same goes for the nebulous "office" where Chandler works, the acting gigs Joey lands on shows that don't really exist, the way Phoebe supports herself despite being unemployed and recently homeless. None of it is real, so all of it is possible.

- You and your friends rarely interact in any meaningful way with anybody aside from one another. When you do, those are other ghosts.

Rachel, I would dearly love for you and your friends to ascend to the next place, to go into the light, to do whatever needs to be done. I think knowing that you're dead is a big step in that direction. In the meantime, if you need to hang around Central Perk, that's okay. Everyone is too frightened of the orange couch to ever sit on it. I tried to move it out once and it emitted a deep Satanic growl so I just left it.

I'm sorry no one told you life was going to be this way. Your job's a joke, you're broke, your love life is literally D.O.A.

Gunther

James Taylor

March 15, 2004

Dear Friends,

As you know, I've always been there for you over the years. Due to circumstances that have proved overwhelming, however, I regret to inform you that, as of July 1, I will no longer come running when you call out my name.

I realize this comes as a shock to some of you, especially those who seem to have had occasion to call out my name several times a day, thus forcing me to come running with great haste. While I hope that you will still think of me as a friend, I know it will be a blow to not have me at your disposal. You may be angry. But this change in policy must take place.

When I originally recorded "You've Got a Friend," in 1971, it was meant to reach a select audience of people to whom I was actually very close. Having been endowed by my secret alien parentage with certain abilities (super speed, ultra-hearing, a pleasant singing voice, and a loving nature), I decided to use my powers for good and provide assistance to others in the form of a sort of "super friendship." While other superheroes chose to fly, catch bank robbers, patch up dams, and the like, I decided that James Taylor would be the most powerful and loving friend this world had ever known. And, hopefully, maintain a successful recording career at the same time in order to pay the bills and have a creative outlet.

The plan worked well. The song became a hit, selling millions of copies, and was distributed around the world. Since it was a song from my heart (even though Carole King wrote it), I was pleased by its success. I hoped that listeners would think of it as a sentiment to be shared between two friends, neither of which would necessarily be me.

For the most part, that was the case. But soon there emerged a growing group that cracked my code, realizing that "You've Got a Friend" was not just a song but an implicit contract. Almost none were really my "friends" to begin with, but they started calling out my name. I would be in the middle of tuning my guitar or making tea in my kitchen at the Martha's Vineyard house and my ultra-hearing would pick up a desperate "James Taylor!" from someone who had just had a fight with their boyfriend, or binged on junk food again, or lost out on a promotion, or needed someone to hold the ladder while they cleaned the gutters, or whatever. When that happened, I would dutifully come running to see them. Again.

For a while, I was fine with this. My superpowers made it all feasible, if a bit time-consuming. I was seeing the world and I really seemed to be helping people. Sure, I never knew the boss or the family member that they were complaining about, so I couldn't give advice really. I just listened (a lot!). That seemed to be what they needed anyway. But by the late '80s, I noticed that my recording career was tapering off. Billy Joel or Christopher Cross would call me up (using the phone, thank goodness) to record something, but I would be too busy responding to a farmer in Iowa calling out my name or a banker in Tokyo who decided to yell "James Taylor!" as loud as he could because he felt "uneasy." And boom, because I was being a friend, I lost out on the gig.

By the '90s, things were clearly out of control, but a deal was a deal. I had told people that I would be there, yes I would. But I was going days without sleeping, eating whatever food I could grab on the road, and rarely seeing my family, who wondered, quite fairly, why I never seemed to be around for them. And it was always the same people calling out my name. Four or five times a day. Occasionally, in desperation, I would bring them puppies or kittens, something else to channel their love to, but they would never get the hint. Free copies of the *Sweet Baby James* album were rarely accepted enthusiastically.

Finally, after a particularly harrowing beginning of 2004, I'd decided that enough was enough. Was it Mrs. S. of Minneapolis who had taken to calling out "James Taylor! And grab some Oreos!"? Might have been. Could have been Mr. F. in Melbourne who screamed my name at two in the morning and then changed his mind when I got there and told me to leave. The entire classroom of first graders to whom Ms. W. taught the "James Taylor trick" certainly didn't help matters. It just wasn't funny. To me, anyway.

But in reality, it's all of these cases. And so many more over so many years. Because while I have been a friend, I don't think most of you know the meaning of friendship. It's a two-way street, and frankly it's time you all learned that the hard way by realizing your actions have consequences. So the deal is off.

As of July 1, if you call out my name, all you'll hear is the sound of your own voice. I will be taking time to work on a new album and touring some colleges in the Northeast with my good friend Art Garfunkel. Between now and June 30, however, the deal still stands, but I do ask you to use it judiciously and perhaps begin to taper off.

Thanks.

Your "friend,"
James Taylor

To: Dana_Scully_FBI@aol.com
From: Fox_Spooky_Mulder@compuserve.com
Subject: The Lost X-Files

....

Scully, I'm pretty sure I'm about to be captured
or killed or something by the government or aliens
or the government working for the aliens or vice
versa. It's hard to tell anymore. Point is: I'm in
danger again. So I need to pass along some really
high-level information, the kind of thing that
people need to know about and that no one can ever
find out about. The truth needs to get out there
and it will endanger everyone and lives will be
saved and/or lost. Anyway.

Here:

1974—1979: The United States and much of the world
is caught up in the disco craze. It involved steady
beats and high-pitched, heavily reverbed vocals.
Also a great deal of dancing and cocaine. The FBI
has evidence that this craze, while initially seen
as a reaction against the heaviness and earnestness
of arena and prog rock music, was in fact a
standard take-over-the-world alien plot. The plan
was to hypnotize the world's population, get them
high on drugs, and then simply kill them all. The
plan was foiled purely by accident when the alien
leaders began hanging out way too much at Studio 54
in New York, partying with Bianca Jagger and Andy
Warhol, and dying of overdoses.

1977: A series of "close encounters of the third
kind" occur in the desert Southwest, leading to odd
and obsessive behavior by people who reportedly

279

witnessed alien crafts. This obsession, in at least one case, leads to the compulsive creation of mashed potato replicas of Devil's Tower in Wyoming where the crafts were believed to be landing. In the end, the entire project was a marketing stunt by the American Mashed Potato Council, who poisoned many Americans with hallucinogenic drugs in order to promote their sickening product.

1983—present: Various companies begin selling water, regular water, in bottles. This despite the fact that you can go right to a sink and fill up any old cup with water that is pretty much the same. Some of the bottles of water eventually cost three dollars or more. People buy it, too, in increasingly large numbers. The Bureau has come to believe the theory that there is a virus at work here wherein the public presence of one water bottle compels otherwise sane people to go out and acquire bottles of their own, even though, again, tap water is always available. As for where this all comes from, it may be a cabal of industrialists, it may be Chinese mystics, or it may just be that people are kind of dumbasses.

1985: Duran Duran suddenly stops being popular, which makes no sense. You remember them, right, Scully? The earlier stuff was great, "Girls on Film," "Rio," and all that. But *Seven and the Ragged Tiger* is a really underrated album. I guess they lost some chemistry after Andy and John did Power Station while Simon and Nick split off to make the Arcadia album. Still, you'd think the real fans would stay with them. Yet, I'm one of the only ones who did. What's up with that? Theory: the Pentagon is somehow involved.

1990: A dog near Phoenix acts weird all day and then returns to normal. Unsolved.

1997: A huge influx of Sasquatches (aka Bigfoots) is reported in the Pacific Northwest. The beasts are said to be well over six feet tall, hairy, and constantly emitting a powerful stench. Investigations reveal that for the most part, these Sasquatches are members of the Seattle Supersonics NBA basketball team. In particular, Shawn Kemp, Jim McIlvaine, Detlef Schrempf, and Steve Scheffler. The players would don ornate disguises immediately after games when their body odor was strongest and roam the countryside of suburban Seattle just to freak people out.

Ultimately, the players were abducted by actual Sasquatches with whom they actually fell in love and mated. The NBA soon had to deal with the competitive threat that these half-human, half-Sasquatches posed to the league. They were all well over seven feet tall and had the innate rebounding instinct that we know is common among Sasquatches.

The progeny were kidnapped and raised in captivity by the Bureau. When they grew to adulthood, they were shaved and sent to play in overseas leagues. Trying to prevent such cross-breeding in the future, the NBA relocated the Seattle franchise to Oklahoma City, which is relatively Sasquatch free.

Oddly, after retiring from the NBA, Kemp, McIlvaine, Schrempf, and Scheffler moved into the woods, reuniting with their Bigfoot brides.

1999: Jesse Ventura is elected governor of Minnesota.

2001: A reported alien presence said to be terrifying beach areas in Louisiana turned out to be a pelican. To be fair, pelicans are freaky looking, Scully.

2003: Ventura leaves office and Arnold Schwarzenegger is elected governor of California.

Look, Scully, maybe you shouldn't investigate this one too closely. Some things are better left unknown. Let the truth just stay out there.

Mulder

October 12, 1960

Mr. Hohoff,

I am delighted, as I know you are, with the success of the book and I am eager to begin a new novel that I can get out to the public as soon as possible. I am absolutely bursting with ideas and feel the name "Harper Lee" will be synonymous with prolific writing for generations to come. "Harper Lee has ANOTHER book out ALREADY?" That's what people will be saying.

Here's my first notion and I am prepared to start work on it right away:

Boo Radley: Time Cop. The reclusive Mr. Radley, who emerges, however briefly, from the shadows at the end of *Mockingbird*, is revealed to not really be a shut-in after all but rather a top officer in the Interchronological Police Squadron! Once he gets his orders, he climbs in his time machine (located in his house, that's why no one is ever allowed in there!) and blasts off to ancient Egypt, Victorian England, or whenever. His mission: stop time-traveling criminals—generally by stabbings staged to look like accidents as in *Mockingbird*—from altering the proper course of history.

I await your approval.

Ms. Lee

* * *

July 8, 1961

Mr. Hohoff,

No traction on that last idea, huh? Okay. How about this:

To Surf a Mockingbird. Tired of living in the repressive South,
Atticus, Jem, and Scout set out for sunny California! Atticus becomes
a level-headed surf champion and defends minority surfers from
charges of breaching surf protocol. In the end, when the bad guys
die of unexplained knife wounds as Atticus's children hide nearby,
the deaths are chalked up to simple accidents.

Note: this might work as a movie as well. Frankie Avalon as
Atticus?

Ms. Lee

* * *

February 21, 1974

Mr. Hohoff,

Just wanted to let you know I'm still brainstorming. I'm just going to
say the title and see what you think:

TO BE KILLED BY MOCKINGBIRDS

People like horror. *The Exorcist* was huge. So it's years after the
first book. Jem has moved away. Atticus has died, and without his
presence and expert marksmanship to worry about, the people of
Maycomb finally let out their pent up aggression on the now grown-
up Scout with threats and vandalism and all sorts of cruel acts.

Finally, she can take it no longer and uses her MAGICAL ABILITIES to summon forth great clouds of mockingbirds to attack and kill the racist people of Maycomb!

See, there's, I don't know, a witch or something in Maycomb who gave her special powers as a thank you to Atticus for defending her in a witch hunt. Yeah, that'll work. Or maybe Scout just fell and hit her head in the woods and when she woke up she could control mockingbirds and the head injury screwed her up a little, so she's VENGEFUL. In truth, I haven't really worked this part out. But I will!

Anyway so she's being harassed by the townspeople.

"It's a sin to kill a mockingbird, but for me it's a blessing for you to be killed by a flock of mockingbirds!" Scout shouts as millions of bloody-beaked birds swarm around her, following her every command. "YOU'RE ALL SINNERS!"

Then the killing really kicks in. Tippi Hedren ain't got nothing on this carnage.

RIGHT?

Ms. Lee

* * *

May 27, 1977

Mr. Hohoff,

I just saw *Star Wars*. How about *To Kill a Space Mockingbird*? Not really formed yet. Just a thought.

Ms. Lee

June 19, 2011

Mr. Hohoff,

Okay, I think I better just let the Mockingbird thing rest. Been trying for decades and just getting nowhere.

I am pleased however to be writing again, this time under the pseudonym E. L. James, whose first book, *Fifty Shades of Grey* will be published tomorrow. Wish me luck!

Ms. Lee

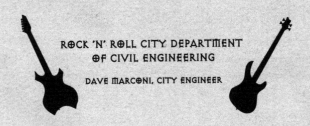

ROCK 'N' ROLL CITY DEPARTMENT
OF CIVIL ENGINEERING

DAVE MARCONI, CITY ENGINEER

Dear Mayor Slick,

We shut down another overpass today. It was near collapse. I have
to tell you I'm getting a lot of angry phone calls, people freaking
out about our crumbling municipal infrastructure. All I can do is
ask them, "Don't you remember? We built this city . . . we built this
city on rock 'n' roll?" Hey, I know those were wild times back when
we did that, and I agree that it seemed like a really good idea at the
time. But rock 'n' roll, really any musical genre, is no foundation for
a major metropolitan area. It was a terrible decision and the consequences are becoming increasingly dire.

Are you familiar with the civil engineering term "hoopla," Ma-
dame Mayor? It's a slang term meaning raw sewage. Parts of the city
are now knee-deep in hoopla. This is because instead of installing
standard pipes and valves and the kind of equipment other cities
use, we installed electric guitars and amplifiers. It doesn't even make
sense. Those things can't carry sewage. The fact that we were pretty
high when we made these decisions is an explanation, but it is certainly not an excuse.

The real question is how are we going to address this problem
and find solutions? As I've said before, there are major corpora-

tions who could step in and rebuild our city. But when I suggested that, you laughed it off saying that there were too many corporation games and that corporations are always changing their names. Mayor Slick, as long as they can do something about the hoopla spilling over our guitar string-based sewer network and flooding the streets, I think they can call themselves whatever they want.

Even outside of the hoopla, the city is a mess. The zoning board is dominated by prog rockers, which is a nightmare because there needs to be a "concept" even to build a dang office park. Councilman Alan Parsons is always demanding funding for his various projects. The electric grid is now firmly under control of Councilman Van Halen's cabal and a total disaster because all he wants to do is "crank things up." The fire department is run by Gothabilly musicians, which I don't even know what that is.

Look, I think we can get by for a little while and make some improvements. Just, I beg you, don't let anyone know what we've done here. Let's keep a lid on it. I'm told that you've actually formed a band with members of the city council, and I urge you not to address this issue in song because from what I can tell, you're pretty terrible.

Thanks,

Dave Marconi

P.S. Someone has ordered all the airplanes at the airport to be replaced by starships. And I can't even . . . you know what? I quit.

REJECTED

SUPER HALFTIME SHOW BOWL

PROPOSALS

SUPER BOWLS XLVI TO XLVIII

SUPER BOWL XLVI—FEBRUARY 5, 2012

- With the third "Dark Knight" movie about to arrive, DC Comics submitted a proposal for a "Battle of the Batmen" halftime show that would feature not just current Batman Christian Bale, but former Batman portrayers Adam West, Michael Keaton, Val Kilmer, and George Clooney. While it might have been fun having the actors, all in their respective Batman costumes, compete in verbal or physical skills competitions, the plan as proposed was something far more grim: just fighting. That was it. West, Bale, and all in between punching and kicking each other, trying to win an actual fight. DC Comics added a parenthetical that perhaps butterfly knives, nunchuks, and billy clubs could be placed randomly around the field.

- Madonna was hired. The Committee jotted down idea of "Battle of the Madonna Personae" for possible future use.

SUPER BOWL XLVII—FEBRUARY 2, 2013

(No proposals received, Mayan apocalypse expected)

- Beyoncé!

SUPER BOWL XLVIII—FEBRUARY 2, 2014

- Proposal received to play off the fact that the game takes place
  on Groundhog Day. In a tribute to the central plot device of the
  movie *Groundhog Day,* all living players of the previous forty-seven
  Super Bowls would be forced to replay their games over and over,
  with forty-seven games taking place on the field simultaneously.
  Players who played in multiple Super Bowls would have to play
  those games at the same time. The play would continue until such
  time as each player learned to care more about others than himself,
  much as the Bill Murray character did in the film. Proposal was
  rejected because all football players are already completely selfless
  and loving individuals.
- Though it wasn't technically a proposal in the traditional sense,
  the Grambling State Marching Band showed up outside league
  headquarters and played Peter Gabriel's "In Your Eyes" to league
  executives to try to recapture the magic they once had together.
- Singer Bruno Mars was selected. The Committee voted to try to
  trick Mr. Mars into wearing a Grambling State Marching Band
  uniform.

Acknowledgments

Thank you to Jill Moe and to all my family for their support and patience. Thanks as well to Peter Clowney, Larissa Anderson, Bill Radke, Dave Eggers, John Hodgman, John Warner, Mauro DiPreta, Jennifer Gates, Matt Inman, Patton Oswalt, Paul F. Tompkins, Caissie St. Onge, Gabriel Roth, Brian Cronin, Mike Rylander, Martin Bell, Nina's Coffee Cafe in St. Paul, John Munson, Janey Winterbauer, Steve Roehm, Joe Savage, Richard Medek, Bill Corbett, Kevin Murphy, Rick Moe, Jason Isbell, and Dave the dog, all for reasons.

About The Author

JOHN MOE is the host of Minnesota Public Radio's nationally syndicated show *Wits*. He is also the author of "Pop Song Correspondences," a column on McSweeneys.net. He lives in St. Paul, Minnesota.